‖‖ ‖ ‖‖‖‖‖‖‖ ‖ ‖‖ ‖‖ ‖‖‖‖‖‖‖ ‖‖‖

W9-DEE-619

This book is for men **and** women. Men learn many of these home remodeling skills from their dads, same as their dads learned from **their** dads. Women though, are becoming more self-reliant and are quite capable of doing most of the repairs men do - in many instances - with **more** care and skill. My part is to make it easier for everyone, and to help **you all** save money.

I've been with **NEWSRADIO 740 KTRH** over 6 years now and talking with tens of thousands over my radio programs answering as many questions as time allows. It isn't always easy to get an open line and we seem to run out of time often. So, in this book, I've listed the most often asked questions and I give the answers.

Just look at the chapter heading and turn to the correct page. If what you want answered is not in the book, call (713) 526-4740 during my weekend programs and I'll give you the answers. Then, I'll put your question(s) in my **next** book.

To my fans, I want to thank you for listening to my radio broadcasts, for sending so many nice letters, and for suggesting that I write a book. Because of you I got a raise, I'm able to better care for my family, and I took time off to write the book. I hope you enjoy it.

Tom Tynan

HOME IMPROVEMENT

With

TOM TYNAN

SWAN PUBLISHING
TEXAS ● CALIFORNIA ● NEW YORK

Author: Tom Tynan
Publisher: SWAN Publishing
Editor: Pete Billac
Layout Artist: Sharon Davis
Cover Designer: Glen Clark
Cover Photographer: Gary Bankhead

First Printing, December 1993
Second Printing, January 1994
Third Printing, March 1994

@ December 1993
Tom Tynan and SWAN Publishing
Library of Congress Catalog Number 93-087087
ISBN 0-943629-11-X

All rights to this book are reserved. No part may be reproduced or translated by any means, electronic or mechanical, including photocopying, recording, or by any information, storage or receival system without written permission from the author and publisher.

HOME IMPROVEMENT WITH TOM TYNAN is available in quantity discounts through: SWAN PUBLISHING COMPANY, 126 Live Oak, Ste. 100, Alvin, TX 77511 (713) 388-2547

Printed in the United States of America

Dedication

To my children, Jimmy, John and Amanda. If it wasn't for you three, I wouldn't work at all.

INTRODUCTION

I was driving to a local home improvement sales center one Saturday morning to buy drain pipes, and couldn't decide whether to choose the tin or the plastic type. I'd get advice from the salesperson and then decide.

I turned on the car radio to hear news, sports or music. The first button I pushed was KTRH 740 and the discussion just happened to be on the subject of drain pipes. The man talking said to buy neither, that a new type of rain **filter** was what I should get. I had heard the program before but usually switched to anything else. How to fix a toilet or what kind of paint to put on your house was boring. But not this time, it was something that involved **me** and the timing couldn't have been better.

As I listened to that friendly voice over the air waves, I was impressed at the knowledge that flowed so freely as well as the tone and casual demeanor of the host. I was actually **enjoying** listening to this guy answer questions on **home repair!** Nobody would believe this! **I** didn't believe it!

But, in the next 15 or 20 minutes, I became a fan of **Tom Tynan.** I listened to his show three weekends in a row, Saturday and Sunday. I even taped them. As I played the tape back to **really** listen, I discovered that Tom has a way of making even home improvement information interesting **and** fun. He is also believable, and his audiences seem to adore him.

I wrote to Tom telling him that I thought he should write a book and that my company would be interested in publishing it. I knew it would be good if he could write the way he sounded. Within the week I got a phone call from Tom telling me he was interested.

We needed to meet face-to-face to discuss the details. He and I live light-years away so we made plans to rendezvous at a restaurant mid-way. *"How will I know who you are?"* he asked. *"I'll be in faded jeans and a blue shirt and carrying a book under one arm,"* I said.

*"How will I know who **you** are?"* I queried. *"I'm short, fat and bald,"* he laughed. *"I'll meet you at the reception area. I'll be there at 11:30 or before. I'm never late."*

I arrived a few minutes late because of traffic, and Tom was already there. The first thing I noticed was a wide, sincere smile. He was neither short nor fat. I met a young, 35-year-old man, who was over 6 feet tall, 185 athletic pounds, and handsome. He is losing hair but it's something you don't notice - not on him, anyway.

Let me tell you about Tom. You can *"feel"* his presence. He exudes self-assurance and he is extremely personable. He is a *real* person, and is not aware of his celebrity. He doesn't look around, you know, like many new celebrities do to see if anyone recognizes them. Not a lot of people know his face but many know his voice. With the rising popularity of his new television show, **Our House,** now being shown around the country on several networks, this will change. I don't think it will change Tom.

VIII

His radio show, **KTRH Home Improvement HotLine,** airs each Saturday and Sunday from 11 am to 2 pm and is "the" most listened to home improvement show in Texas on those two days. A direct quotation from the station about Tom and his show is:

"Designed to aid novice do-it-yourselfers, as well as seasoned veterans just needing a pointer or two, the no-nonsense advice of KTRH Home Improvement HotLine host TOM TYNAN has earned listener respect. Tom is a graduate architect, teacher, home builder and recognized member of the construction industry. Listeners get easy-to-understand tips necessary to tackle any home project like the pros. Topics range from home building and remodeling to electrical wiring and plumbing repair to sheetrock and roofing."

There's more to **Tom Tynan** other than his business credentials. Tom is a family man; he has three children, Jimmy 5, John 3, and Amanda, 1. His wife, Jennifer, is going to school to be a Physician's Assistant. He is a loving father, a devoted husband, a good Christian, and a tireless worker. He is career-oriented, and loves what he does. In fact, he loves it so much that he is no longer active in the construction business although it was extremely lucrative.

Tom voices his opinions honestly and without reservation. He will go head-to-head with anyone who questions the validity of his advice or suggestions. He also "marches to his own music" and "tells it like it is" on material, workmanship, warranties and appliances. Those of you who have heard even **one** of his shows can verify that. If you meet him, you'll like him immediately. I did.

The way he sounds over the radio is the way he is; charismatic, candid, truthful and outspoken. Apparently, it has worked in his favor. The average number of adults 25 years old or older who listen to each **quarter-hour** of his show on Saturday is almost **25,000.** And that's in Houston only. NEWSRADIO 740 KTRH is powerful and can be heard from **Brownsville,** Texas to **Baton Rouge,** Louisiana.

On **Sunday,** the time when people are in church, fishing, playing golf, sun bathing, snow skiing or sleeping, Tom Tynan's listening audience is almost **20,000** adults 25 years or older during **each quarter hour** of his program. And this too, is in the Houston area alone. The surprising statistic is that on Saturday, almost **60%** of his listeners are **female.** And on Sunday, more than **half** are female!

There's much **more** I could share with you about the author of this book but we have to save some for his second book. This information I've shared with you should be sufficient to impress you. It impressed **me!**

Yes, **Tom Tynan** is a special individual. Those of you who listen to his radio broadcasts will enjoy his writing; he writes just the way he talks, in plain, easy-to-understand language. It's difficult to write a personality into home improvement questions but somehow, Tom has managed to do that too. How in the world can anyone make listening to home repairs enjoyable? Tom does, doesn't he?

Pete Billac
Editor

TABLE OF CONTENTS

What homeowners are saying about Tom Tynan

Outstanding book! Easy to read and easy to understand. One chapter alone saved me $600 and a lot of headaches . . .
Rudy Hebert, San Antonio, TX

My husband Bob and I both enjoy listening to Home Improvement Hotline every Saturday and Sunday on KTRH. Tom Tynan is terrific and his book is fantastic! It will help us save money and do our home repairs correctly . . .
Karen Cucchia, Stafford, TX

This book is good! The guy makes reading about an otherwise boring subject, interesting and enjoyable. Reading only one chapter saved me several thousand dollars . . .
Gene Mathews, Lafayette, LA

I always listen to Tom Tynan on the radio. He respects the fact that women as well as men, care for and maintain their home. He has a personality that is effervescent . . .
Alice Torres, Beaumont, TX

I've been a builder for over 30 years and I get KTRH here in Baton Rouge. I enjoy listening to Tom Tynan. He's knowledgeable and accurate and a great asset to honest homebuilders . . .
Gene Buckel, Denham Springs, LA

My favorite program on my favorite station. I have actually "learned" to be handy from Tom Tynan's program. I've listened to it faithfully for over 5 years . . .
Elvia Menandez, Brownsville, TX

I thoroughly enjoyed his new book, Home Improvement. I bought 5 copies and I'm looking forward to his next book, whatever it will be. I'm a structural engineer and the guy makes sense. He tells it like it is and I really like that . . .
    Alvin Davis, Austin, TX

I enjoy listening to Tom. He tells you things in plain words and he is not afraid to go against material or procedures that he knows are wrong. I respect his judgment. I met him at a homeshow and he is just a regular guy . . .
    Melvin Leva, Kingwood, TX

The guy is terrific! I'm amazed at all he knows. Some people ask questions that are really difficult and he just rattles off an answer, in detail, without hesitation. I listen to his program all the time. I want a dozen of his books . . .
    Dr. Carl Bechtel, Webster, TX

I do all sorts of home repairs and I thought I was pretty good at them. I listen to Tom Tynan to make certain I do things right. He's fun listening to and he knows what he's talking about . . .
    Ben Weir, Alvin, TX

Tom makes the book fun to read and he also tells so much that will end up saving everyone money. I hold him in high regard . . .
    Don M. Polensky, Victoria, TX

*I took Tom up on his disclaimer (page 127). I'm a chemist and told him to use only **mineral oil** to coat a butcher block. I thoroughly enjoyed the book and I feel he has the best home improvement show I've ever found. I've learned a lot from him . . .*
    Dan Kelsey, Fulshear, TX

** Steve Hill of Sugarland, Texas bought **15** of Tom's books before he even saw one. Thanks Steve. Hope you enjoyed getting those two bonus books and had a great Christmas.*

This is the **third** printing of **Volume 1** in three months. The response has been overwhelming and the comments so positive that we are already planning a **fourth** printing. The book simply saves everyone money and is enjoyable to read.

Tom's next book, **Volume 2** in his six-book series, deals with remodeling any part of your home such as adding a den, fireplace, bath, kitchen, patio, etc. It also gives excellent advice to those of you who are **building** a new home. It's titled **BUILDING AND REMODELING,** and will be in print around the first of April.

Tom is grateful to each of you who bought his book and helped make Christmas for him and his family even merrier. We, the publishers, thank you too.

CHAPTER ONE

How To Screen Your Repairman

The title of this chapter could very well be, *A HOMEOWNER'S WORST NIGHTMARE.* When you even begin to **think** about **calling a repairman,** something is wrong! Next, you have to **find** a repairman, find one who knows what he's doing, and one who won't ruin your house. Most homeowners also have a fear of getting "ripped off" because we've all heard so many horror stories about repairmen who do any number of unconscionable things to a naive homeowner.

Calling the repairman is frightening because you just never know what to expect. The repairman most often called is your **Air Conditioning & Heating** specialists, because these are sophisticated and expensive systems and should have regular, professional maintenance. Close behind him is your **Plumber** who repairs leaky faucets, broken water pipes, unclogs drains, replaces your water heater, or fixes your garbage disposal.

Right behind him is your **Electrician.** Believe it or not, an electrician is rarely called and when they are, it's usually to change out light fixtures, because your house was struck by lightning, a problem with a breaker or maybe you want to install some security lights and don't exactly know how to do it yourself.

The fourth repairman to be called is for **Major Appliances.** The "rule of thumb is": *If you have a Westinghouse washer and it breaks, call a Westinghouse man. If you have a GE, Hotpoint, Kenmore, etc., call the person who deals with **that** particular appliance.*

When a repairman shows up at your door, use your natural instinct, some common sense and **look him over!** Let's say he hasn't shaved in a few days, he smells like a grizzly, he gives you a toothless smile and he is scratching! You look past him at his dent-covered truck and you notice a smoking tailpipe held up by coat hanger wire, the motor is running because if he kills the engine he'll need a "jump", oil is leaking all over your driveway from someplace under his truck, the front windshield is obviously held together by duct tape, his gum-chewing girlfriend in the front seat gives you a patronizing wave, and a junk-yard dog hanging out of the broken driver-side window is barking.

Your mind goes blank. Then, you think of everything that could go wrong. *"I can't let this guy in my house, he smells awful. He'll probably ask if his girlfriend can come in too. Will that dog ever stop barking? He'll ruin whatever he tries to fix. He doesn't look like he knows what he's doing."*

My comment is, "If it **walks** like a duck, **quacks** like a duck, and **looks** like a duck, chances are it **is** a duck!" If you are uneasy with the appearance of this repairman and his truck, dog, girlfriend, tell him whatever was wrong is fixed, even if your house is about to flood from the ceiling because the evaporator coil on your air conditioner is stopped up and your drip pan overflowed. You need repairs now but **not** from this guy. It takes guts but, **pass him up!**

Other than the scenario I drew with this frightening cretin at the door, an obvious "nightmare" and an accident about to happen, let's say another guy comes over who doesn't look so good either. He's pretty dirty, doesn't smell very fresh, but his truck is clean and he seems polite.

As far as **looking** dirty, maybe he's been working hard in dust and dirt and sweating. You might not smell too swift either if you had been crawling around through a hot attic for a few hours. Besides, you're not going to **date** the guy, invite him to have lunch with you at the club, or introduce him to your daughter. He might be a hard-working stiff with a family to support. Look at other things.

Did he show up on time? Did he introduce himself? Show you his business card? Take his hat off when he spoke? Ask you what the problem was? If he did and you let him come inside, did he have a "no-nonsense" approach? Go right to the problem? Invite you to look and show you what was wrong? Did he tell you what he planned to do about it?

If he doesn't invite you to look with him, ask him to see if you can tag along. *"Will you show it to me so I can see what's going on so I can recognize it if it happens to me again?"* And if he says *"Yeah, good idea, come on up and let me show you."* **Great!** These are **good** signs.

Let's say he diagnosed the problem and says he can fix it. If it's a minor problem, but an emergency one, "go with him" on a ballpark figure. For instance, if he says, "*It might cost fifty bucks, no more than seventy-five*", let him do it, pay him, and be happy. But if it's going to cost several hundred or more, follow up with this.

Ask for **proof of insurance.** He must be covered by *Workmen's Compensation* and *Liability* insurance. Ask them to have a *Certificate of Insurance* sent to you **from** his carrier or insurance company. Do **not** accept a copy he might give to you from his hand to yours; **it's not legally binding!**

Ask him to make a quick call to his insurance agent, and **you** talk to them giving your name and address so they can send you papers of his insurance coverage. This means that **if** he or the company he works for gets in some kind of trouble, like insurance being canceled, or is about to go bankrupt, the insurance company has **your name** in the files and will call you. **Don't** rely on the repairman's word even if they are handsome and you're pushing your daughter out of the woodshed to meet him. Period!

Ask for references! Personal references are the best. Does he work on your mother's AC system? Has he done work for your neighbor? Is he a friend of the family or a friend of a friend whom you trust? These are important. If he gives you names, they might be legitimate and they might not. Call them, but know that he wouldn't give out names of people unless they will say good things.

Another way to check his references is find out the place where he **buys his materials!** Call the company, ask for their *credit department* or *bookkeeper,* and ask **them** if he pays his bills on time. They will usually tell you, **especially** if he is a problem or owes them a lot. Yeah, they're happy to tell you because they know he'll be back trying to get more material "on the cuff" and maybe not ever paying them. If he doesn't pay them, it could mean he doesn't have any money. Then, chances are he uses **your** money to pay these back bills and can't fund your job.

If he checks out up to this point, find out the type of **warranty** he offers. On repair work, the minimum warranty is **one year**; not 30 days or 60 days or 90 days, **one full year** and that is a **full warranty**, labor **and** materials.

When he gets to where he diagnoses your problem and tells you what it is, ask him to **put it in writing** and make certain he spells out the material in his estimate - with prices!

It's wise to also **check for a license,** you know, to make certain they are qualified to repair what they say they can repair. This license number should be displayed on their vehicle, on their letter heads, business cards and they might even have a copy of it in their wallet. Many states don't require a license but in Texas, plumbers, electricians and air conditioning repairmen, a license is required!

I know, when something breaks, and you're in a hurry to have it repaired and you might be near panic and not check these people out to this degree or maybe you're afraid they'll walk off on you. If they do, **let 'em** and know you just saved a **lot** of money because the guy would have caused you more problems than you have now. Be smart, take the time and check them out.

No advances! My experience with paying "up front" money is that you might not ever see that person again. **Never** pay until the job has been completed. Follow my rules for checking them out and check what they have done **before** you pay.

THINGS TO WATCH OUT FOR:

First, **if** the guy looks good, and **if** he talks with a degree of knowledge, and **if** you let him into your home, explain what your problem is and look for his reaction. **If** he tries to **scare** you like "*Oh, this is a BIG problem!*" Or, "*Whoa, this is REALLY going to cost you!*" or, "*We'd better shut this or that off immediately!*", or "*This sounds serious*", or "*This could be very, very dangerous*", he has just hoisted the first red flag. This doesn't mean, however, that what he's saying is **un**true, just be aware that it might **not** be true and look for further signs of scare tactics.

Or, **if** he goes around searching for and pointing out other problems like, "*Oh, I think you have termites*", or "*Your attic needs more ventilation,*" Hey, this guy is there to fix your **air conditioner** and not do roofing or venting or pest control inspection.

Beware of this type because they want to make a big "score" on an unsuspecting person. What he's probably doing is trying to be an expert in **everything** and he is probably not an expert at **anything!**

Then, there are the real "smoothies" who offer you things that are **too good to be true.** *"This might cost a little more but you'll never have to call me again in this lifetime. It'll last forever!"* Be wary or words like **"Free, Today's Special,** *I give you my* **personal** *guarantee, or a large pizza if you sign* **now!**"

I'm telling you these things not to insult your intelligence, but because they **happen** each and every day to many; dumb and smart alike. Do **not** let this happen to you! Who is he anyway? What validity can be placed on his **personal** guarantee?

Many of you, I know, will **not** check and will **be** frightened or "conned". I realize this seems like *overkill* in checking but trust me, it's worth the time and effort. I get sick to death when I hear horror stories about widows and grandmothers getting ripped off by some of these home improvement jerks. **Check them out!**

I know it takes some time to do all that I recommend but it's only **one time** for each repair person. This time, can't be compared to the stress and/or expense you'll have if you **don't** check. This isn't a problem **each** time, only the **first** time and when you have a list in your files of good repair people, the next time it's a snap. In fact, take some time **now** and ask your friends, neighbors and family for recommendations for various maintenance and repair contractors and have a list ready for when you need it. And, sooner or later, you will!

HOME IMPROVEMENT GIMMICKS:

I hate these people with a passion. I know it isn't healthy to hate but I make an exception in this case. I have listened to literally **thousands** of good, sweet, *naive* folks over the past 15 years who had been **cheated out of their life savings** or actually **put on the street** because of unscrupulous sales people who suck them dry like a vampire.

The problem is, these scum of society are **everywhere!** And someone is getting hurt by them this very minute as I write about it and again this very minute that you are reading about it. There **are** laws to protect you, but they are not **stringent** enough, nor do they cover **all** the problem areas, and these "criminals" know all the rules. I want you to be aware of some of their gimmicks.

(1) Never buy any type of home improvement from anyone who comes **soliciting** at your door! They usually work in pairs with the "front" man knocking on your door. They know how to do it. This front man will not try to **sell** you anything; his job is only to get his "closer" in to talk to you and **they** do the selling. Far too many people actually **believe** this closer is their friend. He is not!

(2) Never buy any type of home improvement from someone who **calls you on the telephone!** Most of the time it's what is called a "boiler room" operation where people are hired to make phone calls. They get a minimum hourly raise and earn a **bonus** when they lure in a sucker to agree to an appointment with who? **The closer!** The same smooth-talking guy whose front man knocks on doors to get him in to fleece the unsuspecting, has now become **automated!** Same pig, different sty.

(3) Never buy **any** type of home improvement with a **discount coupon!** Let me give you an example, and this doesn't include the ads in area newspapers or telephone books where small businessmen **sincerely** give you $10 off a house call to look at your TV or check your washer or dryer when it breaks. I'm talking about **major** work on remodeling your home.

It takes a substantial amount of money to open any business. And repair and maintenance people - the ones who are reputable - don't try to sell you what you don't need, or try to frighten you into buying something you can't use or offer you **free** things. They simply cannot **remain** in business if they don't charge a fair price for their services.

There is **no way** a repairman can buy a truck, insure it, buy license for his profession, maintain that vehicle, and feed his family by **giving** you anything; they **have** to charge! And, when someone approaches you with **free** this, or **free** that, or a big discount for "buying today" or because "they like your looks," it has to be a gimmick.

(4) Never buy a home improvement that you don't need! Don't consent to buy something you don't want, or can't use.

If you want to **get rid** of a solicitor who knocks or calls to sell you home improvements, just tell them you don't own the home, you're **renting**. They'll do an about-face or hang up the telephone as quickly as they can.

Most of these home improvement solicitors are out to **get** you! They'll give you a free TV, or pay off an existing loan and ask you to mortgage your home to get this loan. They'll write a deal promising you that, *"Your house will be done **free** - if you let us use it to sell other homes in the neighborhood. We won't bother you or even call, only sometimes you'll see people in your yard. Just don't shoot them!"* Sounds appealing, doesn't it.

But, **trust the fact,** that **before they leave,** they'll put a **contract** under your nose for you to sign and if you do, you'll be signing over their right to **take your home** if you are late with a payment for what they said was **free!**

Many of these shoddy home improvement people who sell siding will offer you a **discount** for using your home as a **showplace** because *"They have a deal with the manufacturer on the material."* Their only deal is to **pay** for the material once they get you to sign "For Labor Only" and the charge for this labor is maybe **three times** the cost of labor **and** material combined! They get "zero" free from the manufacturer and you'll get nothing but free **headaches** if you do business with them!

> Don't sign anything! Don't give them any front money! Don't fall for these gimmicks! If you're in doubt, call your **attorney,** call the **cops,** or . . . **call me!**

If you want some type of home improvement, go out and find **them!** Screen them the way I told you, buy what you need, buy what you can **afford,** look for reputable service and repairmen, get at least **two** estimates on any sizable job and **pay a fair wage** for the service. Yes, do it right. It will save you money and grief in the long run.

THE HANDYMAN:

Let me suggest that each person reading my book have a **Handyman.** These folks are relatively inexpensive and can do a myriad of "small jobs" to make your life easier. Whether you're good with "fixing things" or not, there are times when you have other things to do or maybe you need help with a project you choose to do yourself. If so, call your handyman. And, if you find a "good" handyman, **spoil him!** Give him a few extra bucks, a present for Christmas, let his kids fish in your lake, swim in your pool, become **friends!**

A handyman can repair a fence, replace a pane in a window, fix a leaky faucet, install a light fixture, patch a hole in your sheetrock, stop your toilet from dripping, and a host of other small jobs that aggravate even the saintly. But they can't do it all!

What they **shouldn't** do is work on your air conditioning system, tackle complicated electrical jobs, try to work with major plumbing problems, or attempt to work on your large appliances. Too, many won't admit when they **can't** do something because they want to keep their job and/or they want to please you.

With all due respect to good handymen throughout the world, they are **not** trained to work on things that change almost yearly. There are new motors, new codes, new systems and it truly takes a professional to work on them properly. New washers, for instance, have computer chips in them and you need the proper tools and training. I know you'd rather have your handyman do the job and you don't like spending money but you might end up spending tons more if something goes wrong. Too, handymen, usually, don't have any liability insurance.

Where do you find a good handyman? Check with your folks, or your friends. Talk to your neighbors, co-workers or ask around. Look in an area newspaper or bring the subject up at a party. In most supermarkets, there is usually a large bulletin board with all sorts of business cards and notices on it. Many will have listings for a lost or found dog, used lawn mower for sale, maid service, baby sitting, typing and bookkeeping service, roofing, an announcement for a church bazaar and what else? You guessed it, a **handyman!**

If you look, you'll find one. If you can't locate a handyman in the places I've suggested, perhaps you can place a small ad in the newspaper and advertise for one. **Anywhere** you can find one, do it! And screen them the way you screen the other repairmen. In fact, maybe closer because they'll be back often and most have "run of the mill" privileges in and around your home. Try not to be paranoid, but be cautious and be smart.

Ladies, please don't take offense because I say repair**MAN**, work**MAN,** handy**MAN** or anything**MAN**. I realize that many of these are repair**WOMEN** and work**WOMEN** but the majority of these work**PEOPLE** are still, in fact, male.

CHAPTER TWO

Roofing

Q. **When do I need a new roof?**

A. A lot of people think that just because they have a **leak** in their roof they need a **new** roof, and this is just not true. In most cases leaks are generally isolated; most are usually found around joints, and they can be trouble-shot and fixed and the roof can last a long time. Let me explain when you **will** need a new roof.

Shingles have a layer of granules that basically protect them against the elements, and as time and weathering takes its toll, these granules wear off. They wear more towards the bottom of the roofline around the eaves than they do at the top, because as the water drains, it picks up speed and by the time it reaches the bottom, it has the same effect as soil erosion by a river.

Try this. Get a ladder and don't go **on** the roof, just at the lowest point of the roof and see how badly the shingles are worn. Then, take one of the worst looking ones and bend it in two. Is it crispy? Does it break like a fresh cracker? If it's a wood shingle roof, you look to see if the wood has rotted, or if shingles are missing or have fresh cracker? If it's a wood-shingle roof, you look to see if the wood has rotted, or if shingles are missing or have slipped to the side. At this point, go to your files and look for the **warranty** on your roof as well as the roofer who installed it. There's no need to start soliciting bids on a new roof at this point.

> When using a ladder to work on **anything**, I don't need to remind you to **make certain** that ladder is safe, do I? If it's an old wooden ladder, check it for rot and loose rungs. If it's a metal ladder, make certain it's either open all the way, locked in properly, or positioned with sufficient angle so it won't topple over.

Another time to look at your roof is after a bad rainstorm or high winds. Check to see if any shingles are missing. After a hail storm, for instance, shingles get *bruised* and are often *beaten off* by the hail. This might not cause your roof to leak but it will shorten the life of it and insurance companies tend to pay off quickly after a hail storm. Now, don't go out praying for hail but if there **is** damage, call your insurance agent immediately.

There comes a time when **all** the roofs in the neighborhood are being replaced. *"Oh my goodness,"* you say, *"all the neighbors are getting new roofs, guess I need one too!"* And you panic and call a roofer or stop one of your neighbors and ask who is doing their roof. **All** roofers welcome new jobs. If you **tell** a roofer you think you need a new roof, they will probably agree with you. *"Oh yeah,*

> If it is only a **leak**, remember, leaks can be fixed **without** putting on a new roof. If you go up on your roof to check on a leak, don't stomp around on it or drag a ladder, across it. **You** might cause more leaks.

Q. **Should I use 15 or 30-pound felt?**

A. Felt does nothing more than **protect the roof before** the shingles are put on. In other words, you tear the old roof off and you put the felt down quickly to protect from a rain. Once the shingles are on, the felt is worthless to you.

You should use **15-pound felt** on a low-sloped roof if it's only going to be on a day or two before you install new shingles. If you're using thin shingles, it will sit flatter and you want it flat. Nobody wants a lumpy roof. If you have **a steep-pitched roof,** roofers tend to **use the 30-pound felt**, mostly because they have to walk on it and it won't rip as easily.

If you're building a **new home,** get the **30-pound felt** because it might be weeks before the roof is put on and whatever is **under** the roof is protected, somewhat, from the rain. There is no extra work or labor charges for the heavier weight felt; it goes on equally as fast and the heavier paper and costs only a slight bit more. If you're building a house or putting on a new roof, the slight added cost won't even be noticed.

The difference between **15-pound felt** and **30-pound felt** is the **weight** of this felt in a **square**. A **square** is a 10 x 10 foot area of your roof.

Q. If I put a new roof over an existing roof, should I use felt?

A. **No!** Felt is nothing other than organic paper put down for a quick dry-in on your home. If your old roof has worn shingles and you need new shingles, don't put felt **between** the layers. It makes it look lumpy and chances are it would **be** lumpy and wear out quicker.

What you **should** do is **butt the back of the new shingle to the front of the old shingle.** The term used in the roofing industry is "butt and run" which simply means to make it all flat and line up those **new** shingles even with the **old** ones. Always start at the **bottom** and work **up!**

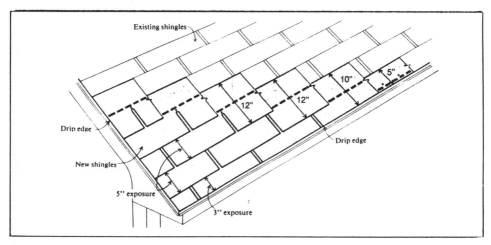

Application of New Asphalt Shingles Over Existing Asphalt Shingles

Read about these "types" of roofs, then go to a nearby home improvement center and look at what's new, and decide which type meets your needs. It isn't necessary to get **expensive** roofing material; they **all** keep out rain and will all last about the same length of time. But, **do** have a **written agreement** with your roofer. A **short pencil** is better than the **longest memory!**

Q. **Can I put a composition roof over a wood shake, or wood shingle roof?**

A. **No!** The reason your wood-shingles are is no longer holding out the rain is because the wood has probably rotted. Do **not** put a perfectly good *(new)* roof over a bad deck. A composition roof over a wood-shingle roof means you would no longer have proper venting. The composition traps more heat and moisture behind it and rots the wood.

The wood-shingle roof is fast-becoming a thing of the past because of fire hazards and new building codes. Too, the new material is safer, stronger, and can look about the same. You are allowed, through a *Grandfather Clause,* to keep a wood-shingle roof but when you need a new one, you are required, in many areas, to use tile, tin or composition; nothing flammable.

In replacing a wood-shingle roof, tear the old wood shingles off and start over again with a solid plywood decking. The deck *(the backing for the shingles)* is one of the most important parts of the roof; it's what the shingles are nailed into. It has to be nailed **tightly** to prevent ripping up during high winds. This plywood decking also helps stabilize your roof and gives your home better structural advantage. It keeps it from **racking** *(twisting and turning in high winds, ground movements, foundation shifting, etc.)* and acts as a diaphragm.

> Wood shingles are still allowed in many areas of the country. The safest thing to do is to check with your *local building department* **before** you begin to build.

Q. **Roofing shingles are sold by weight. Explain these weights to me, and why I should, or should not, use a certain weight shingle?**

A. You'll hear a lot of people talk about 200-pound shingles, and 300-pound shingles, or 365-pound shingles. This doesn't mean a lot to most of us, but it works like this. Shingles are sold by the square. *(Remember? A square is a 10 foot by 10 foot flat area or 100 square feet.)* In that 10 x 10 area, it will have a certain weight, and when someone talks about a 300-pound shingle, it means that - *within that area* - the total weight of the shingles will be 300 pounds, 200 pounds, 365 pounds, etc. Most shingles have gone to fiberglass mats, so the weight doesn't necessarily mean they are better, but now, the new ones are **all** good. The heavier the weight of the shingle, the **thicker** they are and the thicker they **look.**

I'll tell you about the more popular shingles on the market today, **(1)** the **Fiberglass-based** shingle and **(2)** the **Organic** shingle. The organic shingle, sold in the moderate areas of the country, **needs** to be heavier because it has a paper base. The **fiberglass-mat** shingle can be thinner and last just as long as the heavy ones, it just won't look the same. You, make the comparison and decide.

As an example, let's say you're going to buy a 365-pound shingle with a 40-year warranty. These warranties are a joke; your shingle will **not** last 40 years. A 40-year warranty and a 20-year warranty will both last the same length of time - **15 to 18 years max.** You shorten even this life if you have improper venting.

If you want that *wood-shingle **look*** with a fiberglass shingle, go with the heavyweights. If you're not that concerned about it looking **thick**, and want the best value for your money, you can save money by using the lighter weight type of composition shingle.

Warranties on many of these shingle wrappers state that their shingles are **guaranteed** to **last thirty or forty years.** I say "baloney." The only way I would go along with that, is if I could **nail them on the ceiling of my living room!**

Q. **My roofer says I need 30 squares of shingles to cover my roof. Tell me about shingles and how they are sold?**

A. It takes several **bundles** of shingles to make up one **10 x 10 foot square.** Usually, the amount of area a bundle of shingles will cover is marked on the wrapping. If a roofer comes over to estimate a job, he must get **on the roof** and measure the entire flat surface of your roof. If the roof measures, say 25 x 100 feet on each of two sides, this means he has 25 x 100 = 2500 square feet by two or 5,000 square feet total. If a square is 10 x 10 and 100 square feet, this means you divide the 100 into the 5,000 and you need 50 squares of shingles.

The **lighter weight shingles** usually have **3 bundles** to the square, and the **heavier weight shingles**, maybe **4 bundles** to the square. When the shingles are delivered, you can count the bundles and know the actual amount of shingles the roofer ordered. It's important that you count the packages. Some roofers have been known to quote a figure like 26 squares or 30 squares *(depending on the size of your roof)* and far less shingles are delivered. If they aren't delivered, they can't be put on your roof, right? Take a few minutes and check this out. If you do, and the roofer sees this, they are less likely to try anything "funny" on you.

Don't be alarmed if you count a bundle or two **more** shingles than the measurement called for. These are *insurance shingles* against any mishaps and isn't enough money to be concerned over. **Ask** the roofer a few questions anyway. Start off by comparing his figures with your "shingle count" and let him explain what I've already told you. This **keeps** him honest.

Q. **My roof shingles have all kinds of stains on them. Can I clean them off?**

A. Probably **not!** Stains on shingles are usually from **algae** or a **fungus** that grows under the shingles and tend to shorten the life of the shingles. This problem is caused by extreme weather conditions, poor venting of the attic, and the type of shingle. Fiberglass shingles don't stain as much as the organic, another thing to consider when choosing shingles. But, something new!

They are now making **shingles with stain-guard-protection** by adding little metallic pieces of copper, zinc or alloys that actually clean the shingles. If you'll notice under the vent stacks on your roof, you'll see that the lead stacks in your plumbing produce little clean areas shaped like a "V" and the rest is kinda' dark. It's because the lead actually **cleans** the shingles.

Can you get up there with a machine or broom to clean them? **Hardly!** How about Clorox or Purex to kill the algae or fungi? **Doesn't work!** All it does is **dye it white for a while** but as soon as there's a little moisture, the stains come right back. When you look into getting a new roof, choose the type with a **stain guard** that will keep shingles from getting this algae and fungus growth. But **trying to clean your roof is a waste of time** and does nothing other than increase the danger of you falling off the roof. Scientists however, are working on new cleaning solutions daily. I hope they discover a roof cleaner.

Q. I hear so much about VENTING a roof. What types of vents do you recommend?

A. **Venting** a roof is extremely important. An **UNvented** roof will **deteriorate** quickly. It will **ruin** your house, **peel** your paint, **destroy** your insulation, and **cost** you more on energy bills winter and summer. Ventilation is important in the winter in order to **exhaust the moisture** out of your attic. If you don't, you'll have a wet attic and wet insulation is useless. In the summer, venting gets the heat **out.** There are four types of vents on the market.

(1) Power Vents: These hook up to electricity. Stay **away** from vents that run on power because they are on a thermostat and run only when it gets hot in the attic. You need ventilation 12 months a year - all the time - not just **some** of the time!

(2) Turbine Vents: You've seen these on rooftops. They're the ones with the spinning balls on the end and they have been the *old faithful's* of the building industry for a long time. These are good vents and better than what was available before.

(3) Air Hocks: These are little square *passive vents* that are low profile. You've probably seen them on rooftops before and didn't pay any attention. They are tin coverings that fit in a hole cut in your roof, and have coverings to prevent the rain from coming in. They allow your attic to "breathe". They're better than no hole at all - but barely!

(4) Continuous Ridge Vents: At **last**, the building industry has come up with **the very best vent** on the market. They've actually been around for a long time but the old types were ugly, they leaked, and blew off the roof.

The new ones are **remarkable!** They are made of polyethylene, and are covered with a shingle. They are **certified** even in *Dade County Florida*, which has the highest wind certification in the country. They are good in up to 100 mph winds before they start to leak.

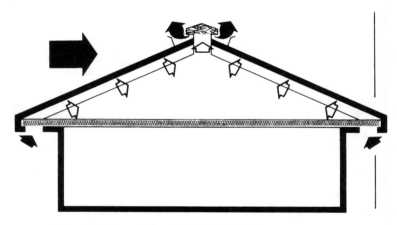

Ridge Vent combined with Soffit Vents

I recommend **Continuous Ridge Vents** on all your ridges, working in conjunction with continuous soffit vents *(vents under the overhangs).* In other words, you have lower vents and upper vents which create an even flow of air. They even ventilate in Alaska. It is the **only way to go** and don't let **anyone** talk you out of it on new home construction or while replacing an old roof.

With 100-mile-an-hour winds, you have **more** to worry about than a slight **leak** in your attic. Your main concern then will be your life, and the lives of your family members.

Q. Someone told me that two layers of roofing adds to my insulation value and will lower my electric bill. Is this true?

A. Only if you're dumb enough to **want** to believe it! What I mean is, only for the *naive.* This book is to help you when buying a home or repairing one you already own. Here's an example: My wife and I went shopping for a house. I don't tell people who I am and most people don't recognize me anyway. We were walking through this house and the owner, who was showing the home, bragged that he had *"Three layers of shingles up there. So, with this extra insulation, his energy bill was very low."* It **sounded** good, but I knew he was wrong.

Follow this closely. Insulation goes against the *skin* of the *conditioned space.* This sounds technical, I know, but what I'm telling you is that your ceiling, if made out of sheetrock, is the **skin**. Your **conditioned space** is where you're sitting. On the other side of that sheetrock is where your insulation is. Your roof isn't on the other side of that **sheetrock,** your **roof** is on the other side of the **attic!** All your roof does is keep the rain, sleet, snow, sun and dust from inside your building.

Think of your roof as nothing more than a hat. If you took that space you were living in and took a little square box and separated it with this great big hat that never touched it, it makes sense that this is **not** insulation, only a **covering to keep out the elements.**

Roofing material is **not** insulation material. With a flat roof, you put insulation **below** the roofing material because it's the only place it will go; there is no attic. But, for a home **with** an attic, one roof is sufficient with proper insulation. Don't let anyone tell you otherwise.

Q. **My roofer says he uses STAPLES to fasten the shingles to the deck. Are staples better to use than nails?**

A. **Never** - not **ever** - allow anyone to use staples to attach your shingles! It's a **terrible** way to go. Because of all these recent high-wind storms doing such damage, the roofing industry has had to re-evaluate what was going on. They **still** won't **say** "Don't use staples," because they don't want to alienate contractors who buy their materials. But I don't care if I make anyone mad as long as I tell the truth. To paraphrase a quotation by Thomas Jefferson, "*The truth is the truth. What you do with it is your own problem.*" That's about as close as I can get to it.

Staples **cut** the shingles. There's no surface-area to hold the shingles down, and during high winds the shingles pull off. In high-wind areas of the country staples are banned. Use roofing **nails** and **hand nail** the shingles. Some roofers use nail guns and it's fine *(if they know what they're doing),* but if the gun sets the nail too deep or not deep enough, there's problems. How can you tell if a roofer is adept with a nail gun? You **never** know without following behind them. I recommend to use nails and to put them in the "old-fashioned way" - with a **hammer.**

Let's talk about how **many** nails should be used on each shingle. Most shingle manufacturers require **four** nails per shingle. In high-wind areas, the insurance industry requires **six!** Roofers in high-wind areas are charging 5 to 6 dollars a square more for six nails. If you're in such an area, pay this extra cost. It's worth it.

Never use staples! I don't care if you put **twenty** of them in one shingle, they will **cut the shingle** and it will **rip right off** in a high wind.

Q. **What kind of a LABOR WARRANTY should I get with a new roof?**

A. We're back to that **warranty business** again, aren't we? Most people, who hadn't read my book, are fooled by these warranties marked on the packets of shingles. Remember, they're bunk! Sounds good though, doesn't it? Your first reaction is, *"Wow! I'll never have to worry about paying for a new roof in **this** lifetime. If it leaks or rots, I'll just call this national company and get a new one."*

But, it doesn't work quite like that, **and even if it did,** these are **material** guarantees. To **take off** the old roof and put on the new one requires a **roofer,** and they aren't free. This brings us face-to-face with yet another warranty.

Most contractors want to give a one or two year, some a 5-year warranty on labor. I would **not** pay for a roof without a **10-year** labor warranty, **period!** If a roofer cannot give you this warranty, find a new roofer who does. That's why it's important to get a **reputable** roofer, not one of these guys who drives by with a truck of material, without an office or insurance and is willing to "make you a deal!" No. You get a **10-year labor warranty - from your roofer!**

If, during this 10-year period, you get a leak here or there, if shingles tear off or just come loose, it isn't such a big deal for the roofer to send out a repair man. But if **you** have to fix it, or call in another roofer, it can cost. No, get that **ten year labor warranty!** As far as the material, expect 15 or 18 years and be satisfied.

Q. **I'm getting conflicting information on the way to treat the VALLEYS. What do you recommend?**

A. For those of you who don't know, the **valley** is where the two planes come together and form a trough. For years, wood-shingles were the things to use. They were the best shingles on the market because, a while back, composition shingles just wouldn't hold up, so you had little choice unless you went to tile or tin.

With a wood-shingle roof you had an exposed metal "valley". *(You've seen them or, you will now because you'll look.)* These were fine at the time, because **this was all there was!** We **had** no choice! But, **when decent quality composition roofing was manufactured,** most roofers switched to the new stuff.

However, **many** roofers **still   used** an open metal valley. What happens, is that you have the edge of your shingle laying **on the metal.** When the **sun** hits this metal, it gets **super hot** and the **shingles bake, get crispy** and **begin to curl.** This drastically shortens the life of your roof.

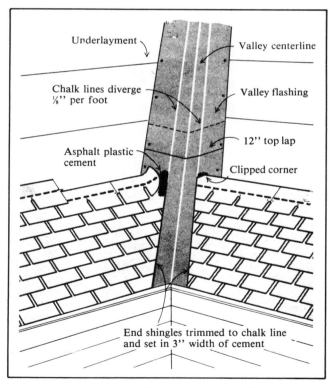

Application of Shingles in Open Valley

There is also something called a **three-tab shingle** which produces a **woven** valley. With the new architectural laminate shingles, these woven valleys are too thick to weave which means a **too thick** valley. Roofers are using what is called a **closed cut valley,** where one layer of shingles run all the way through the valley and **up** the other side. Then, the next plane *(layer)* comes across and they cut a nice straight line along the valley.

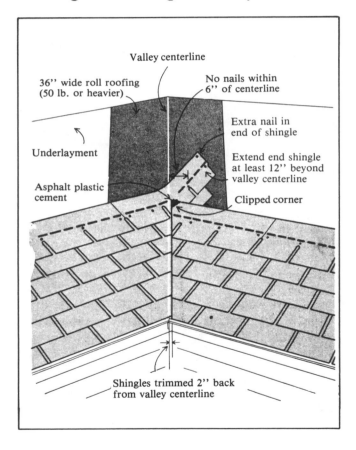

Valley centerline

36" wide roll roofing
(50 lb. or heavier)

No nails within
6" of centerline

Underlayment

Extra nail in
end of shingle

Asphalt plastic
cement

Extend end shingle
at least 12" beyond
valley centerline

Clipped corner

Shingles trimmed 2" back
from valley centerline

Application of Shingles in Closed-Cut Valley

Some of these real stubborn roofers say, *"We'll make it even better and put **tin** underneath and use a closed-cut over the top."* This is **not** good. When you weave **across**, you'll be punching nails **into the metal**, and metal has a tendency to overheat and **bake** the shingles that cover it. Instead of metal, put extra felt, weave the way you're supposed to, and it's all you need.

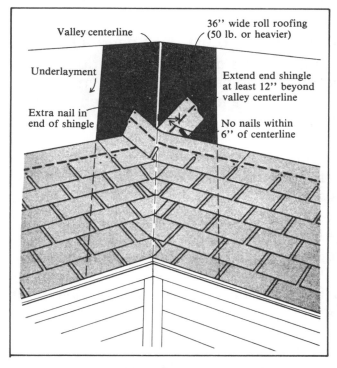

Application of Shingles in Woven Valley

CHAPTER THREE

Insulation

Q. **How do I know if I need to add insulation in my attic? And, what is the "R" value?**

A. You probably **don't** don't need any **more** than you already have. If you **do** need some, do it quickly. This is one upgrade **all** homeowners should make. You can cool *(or heat)* your home more efficiently, and it also saves the environment.

In purchasing insulation, you go a certain **"R" value** to meet the standards for your part of the country. The "R" value is simply the **thickness** of the insulation, and comes in numbers like 30, 38, 42. This is the way you know how much additional insulation you may need. Call your local *power company* for this "R" value information.

When you find your "R" value, go into your attic with a ruler and find how **deep** your insulation is. If you have 6 inches deep of insulation and the power company recommends an "R" value that requires 12 inches of insulation, you need 6 additional inches of insulation. It truly **is** easy and for the amount of savings and efficient cooling and heating you receive, it's well worth the slight effort and expense to do it.

What would you say if I told you how to get **free** insulation? **What? Free?** What do you mean **free?** Nothing is free except, unsolicited advice, the common cold, and something nobody wants. Hold on now, let me explain.

There is about a **5-year payback** on insulation. Whatever the cost is, you'll get **back** over a period of usually five years from the money you **save** on your heating and cooling bill. After that, you continue to save money. So, in effect, the money you save by **having** proper insulation, when you deduct your energy bill savings, it **is**, in fact, **free!**

I'll go into greater detail about this "R" value business. You might not be interested, but it sounds so good and makes me feel important. Technically speaking, the "R" value is . . . **the property the insulation material has, to resist heat transfer.** Heat moves either from inside **out**, or outside **in**, depending if you want to air condition or heat your home.

For instance, you cannot hold cold **in** your house but you can prevent heat from **coming** in. The "R" value is determined by the **difference of temperature** there is from **outside to inside**, and how much **resistance of heat-flow** you need from **out to in** or from **in to out.** Impressed? No, confused, right? Who really cares? Most people don't care **how** it works, only that it **does** work!

When you go to buy a roll of insulation, you'll find two very large numbers on the wrapping. One will give you the "R" value and the other the inches. For instance, **R 11-3 ½ inches** simply means that this insulation is **3 ½ inches thick** and the **"R" value is 11.** After you find out from the power company what your correct "R" value is, and you measure your attic with a ruler, you can determine which to buy. If you **still** aren't sure, the large building supply houses and established hardware stores have people working for them who are knowledgeable. Ask 'em.

When you put this insulation in your attic, **don't pack it down.** It will automatically fluff up. Let it. It **needs** to have the proper "R" value and thickness to work. Don't pack boxes on it or put floors down smashed against it. If you do, you'll compress the insulation and decrease your heating and cooling efficiency.

Q. **Can I add too much insulation? Is more better?**

A. More is **not** better. Since we all live in a variety of climatic conditions, the **more "R" value** you can get with the **thinnest** insulation is best. I don't want to confuse you, but I'll try. For instance, the first six inches of insulation is far more effective than the second six inches. I suggest fiberglass batts in your attic. They come in a large, reasonably light *(though cumbersome)* roll and you don't need any special tools, only a sharp razor knife.

You lug a roll up those hidden stairs, lay it down, and start placing and cutting until it's finished. Then, get another roll and repeat what you did with the first. It's not difficult.

Many catalogs and brochures tout the "R" value telling you that the **higher** the "R" value the greater the **savings.** This is a **lie!** The truth is that the **proper** "R" value gives you the greater savings.

Q. Do I want Cellulose or Fiberglass insulation?

A. **Fiberglass** is best. It's the **only** way to go! **Cellulose** is nothing other than ground up newspaper with additives to make it fire retardant. It has a short life and is cheaper to put in, but holds far too much moisture. Moisture destroys the effect of insulation. Moisture is detrimental to most things and this is why I push the attic vents so much, to get rid of the moisture.

Fiberglass insulation does not break down, it's made to get the highest "R" value for the least amount of thickness, and does not absorb moisture like the cellulose insullation. My recommendation is for **Fiberglass Batts** or fiberglass-batt blankets!

In humid climates, *(snow, heavy rainfall)* my second choice is **blown-in fiberglass**. If you can't get into your attic because the roof is too low, the blown-in type is your logical option. In **dry, arid climates,** the blown-in cellulose is a better choice because it is less expensive, gives you a greater "R" value for the thickness, does the job, and there is not a moisture problem. However, it takes a technician with a machine to install blown-in fiberglass.

Q. **What is a RADIANT BARRIER and how is it applied?**

A. This is new to most people, but has been researched since the early nineteen thirties. It is nothing other than builders **aluminum foil** that come in a roll. It is stapled to the bottom of the rafters, which means when you are standing in the attic it is above your head. The shiny side should be face down *(so you can see it)* and does not have to face the heat source.

These **radiant barriers** work very well in **hot climates.** It should **not be used in colder climates** because it stops the sun's heat radiation from penetrating into the attic. But in the hot, southern climates, the sun is shining and let's say it's maybe 70 or 75 degrees outside. Then when you go **inside**, it's **hotter than** the **outside**. So, you run the air conditioner to pump the heat **back outside** to **cool** the inside. A radiant barrier does not allow your home to absorb all the heat during the day. On hot days, if you go into your attic and feel your insulation, it will be **warm.** With a radiant barrier, it **will not** be warm.

This radiant barrier is applied by being stapled to the bottom of your attic rafters. Staples are okay here, because there's no wind or elements to cause them to tear. Just remember not to block any venting with this material. Let the air flow freely. If you follow these instructions, I promise you'll be more comfortable and your energy bills will be far less expensive.

Q. Will a RADIANT BARRIER destroy my shingles?

A. **No!** This is an old myth. Work done at the *Florida Solar Energy Center at Cape Canaveral (Kennedy)* has shown that you get about a 6 degree difference. What happens is that radiation from the sun penetrates through the shingles, hits the radiant barrier, and since it can't go through, it goes back. The unknowing assume it's going to bake the shingles but this is not so. The radiant barrier gives off only a 6 degree buildup during peak times and 6 degrees is nothing to worry about.

The **color** of the shingle **affects** the **temperature** of the shingle far more than a radiant barrier ever would. For instance, **a black roof gets as much as 20 to 30 degrees hotter** than does a white roof. That's why, in southern areas of the country, you see white roofs and in the snow areas, the darker or black roofs.

Q. I don't have the money to buy insulation. Is there something else I can do to lower my utility bills?

A. **Several things! And inexpensive, too.** It seems the whole world is out there trying to sell us things we don't need. It costs big bucks to buy some of these home improvement items but I'll tell you how and when to cut costs. Insulation is one of the places to begin.

Do this. **Caulk** your windows, and any cracks and areas where you get some infiltration. This costs very little, maybe less than ten dollars, and could save you money. Make certain that your doors seal tightly and if not, get an inexpensive roll of weather stripping to help close the cracks and/or openings. You'd be surprised how **small** an opening it takes to "leak" air or heat.

Also, turn that thermostat **up** a few degrees in the summer and get some **ceiling fans.** In the winter, **lower** that heater a few degrees and wear a sweater inside. I'm not trying to be cute or funny, **wear** some warmer clothing and when you go **outside,** wear more. A few degrees each way can save a you a bucket of money on heating and air conditioning. Then, if you save this money, you can go out and buy the proper insulation.

Q. **I need to add insulation. What I mean is that my present insulation is too thin. Are there some things I need to know before doing this?**

A. **Yes!** When you put additional insulation on top of **existing** insulation, make certain you get the **UNfaced** blankets. You want **no** backing of any type, not paper or plastic or foil - **nothing!** Or, you can get the **blown-in** insulation. If you cannot **find** this type of insulation **without** the backing, get the stuff **with** the backing and then tear the backing off before you put it in. But **never** put additional insulation over existing insulation that has any type of backing or vapor barrier.

Q. I've heard the term VAPOR BARRIER thrown around but never knew anyone to ask about it. What is it and what does it do?

A.   When building a house in northern climates, before the sheetrock goes on the walls, contractors will put polyethylene plastic on the **outside walls** and then put the sheetrock up. This polyethylene plastic is what is knows as a **vapor barrier** because it simply **stops the vapor** from transferring from the inside of the house to the outside. This is but **one** type of vapor barrier. Should you do this in warmer climates? **Absolutely not!**

If you live in a climate where the average **January** temperature is 35 degrees or less, put a vapor barrier on the warm side *(which is the inside)* because you're heating. Many people are putting polystyrene and insulation boards on the **outside** of their home before they put siding up and these act as vapor barriers. This is fine.

But, when you put a vapor barrier on the outside **and** the inside of your home, you've created a *terrarium* in your wall. In other words, it **grows** *things*. It rains, snows and has a mini-climate all its own. When *things* grow in walls, they make you sick. Funguses *(or is it fungi)*, molds, algae, these kinds of problems. Remember *Legionnaire's Disease* that killed people? It was mold and mildew in an **air-conditioner drip-pan** and this causes what is referred to as *Sick Building Syndrome*. This is especially prevalent in hot, humid climates.

A **Vapor Barrier** is one of the most misused products in the United States. You are oftentimes sold things that act as vapor barriers and they literally **destroy** your house. It peels off paint, rots wood and makes you ill and causes "Sick Building Syndrome".

Q. **When I add insulation in my attic, is it okay to cover the electrical boxes?**

A. **Sure!** Cover the electrical boxes *(don't neglect to keep a record of their location)* but **do not cover any recessed lighting!** You need an inch-and-a-half to three inches of air space around these things. If you put insulation over the recessed lighting (we call them *cans* in many cases) you cause a **fire hazard** and can burn your house down. But, you can cover electrical boxes or boxes that house ceiling fans with your insulation.

Q. **I have very little insulation in my walls. Is there a way to add more without tearing the house apart?**

A. Quite frankly, **NO!** You can have insulation **blown** in the walls but it settles to the bottom and there is no guarantee of adequate coverage. To do it properly, you **have** to take your walls apart. If you're remodeling walls, or replacing them, do it then. In northern climates, add this insulation if you put on new siding. Other than these examples, there is no solution.

Sorry, that's the way it is. But it always helps to work on your attic, caulk your windows, weatherstrip your doors, and cover any "leakage" of air. That alone will have to suffice until you decide to change the sheetrock or paneling and **then** add that insulation - **in batts!**

Q. I want to insulate my attic. How do I know how much to buy? What's the best way to measure for it? Is there a trick to this?

A. Believe it or not, there **is** a trick to this and I'm going to share it with you right now. Don't go into your attic and fall through your ceiling or do a tightrope act on each of the ceiling joists trying to measure the area you need insulated.

Do this. In the comfort of your home, go from **room** to **room** - downstairs - and measure. Multiply the length times the width of each room *(a 12 x 14 room = 168 square feet)* and add all the rooms together and buy accordingly. Insulation is sold in rolls that mark the square footage on the wrapping. Simple, eh?

If you have a two-story home, measure the **top** floor only, okay? Just measure the rooms directly **under** your roof; not porches, overhangs, patios, etc. Buy a few square feet extra to get all the spaces. And, be careful in that attic for **whatever** reason you're up there. Make certain it is well lighted and always **watch your step!** Many a homeowner has had to call their sheetrock man to patch a "foot-hole".

Q.   If I have a two-story home, do I insulate between the first and second floors?

A.   **Never!** By insulating **between** these air conditioned or heated spaces, you **trap** the moisture. You need the air to **stratify,** to move up and down freely, to be the same temperature between these cavities. The air would actually stay **colder** in the wintertime if you insulated.

If it's **noise** you need to handle, you know, your bedroom is on the bottom floor and the kids' rooms are upstairs, nail **Homosote** on your upstairs subfloor, then put your padding and carpet on top of that. It will diminish the noise when your kids run, jump or stomp their feet, argue, wrestle or play music, etc. You'll **love** the difference.

I've kept you out of that dusty, dirty attic for **measuring** but now, **somebody** *(either you and/or your helpful neighbor)* will have to go **into** the attic to lay these batts down. Just be careful, okay?. Your kids want to see **Santa** coming down the chimney, **not** their dad through the ceiling. I recommend that each of you take with you **two** 36 x 12 inch boards to move along on between the joists *(they should be 24 inches apart)* so you won't fall through. Kneel on one board and push the other in front so you can advance. Then, reach behind you and pick up the board you just vacated and so on. The job is relatively simple, just take it slow, watch where you kneel or step, and just **be careful!**

CHAPTER FOUR

Plumbing & Fixtures

Q. My tub keeps getting stopped up and I'm spending a fortune on liquid drain cleaners. Isn't there a better way to unblock the P-Trap or unclog my stopped up drain?

A. **Yes!** Every house should have the plumbers best friend. Even when you call a plumber, do you know the very first thing they do? Pull out his best buddy, the almighty **plunger!**

Many people aren't aware of the **trick** there is to using a plunger. First, remove the screen from the drain hole *(use a small screwdriver to take the screw from the middle of the drain)* and put the plunger over the drain hole. Then, **run water in the tub** until the plunger is covered by about two inches. Not the **handle** of the plunger now, the rubber part that makes that *swoosh* sound. If you don't do this water trick, the plunger won't work nearly as well. Then, **plunge, plunge, plunge!**

If this doesn't work, take the plunger out and go to the toilet. In most cases the toilet drain runs through the tub, and from there into the main drain. Now, plunge the toilet, then plunge the tub drain again.

I emphasize to buy a **quality** plunger and you'll only have to do it **one time** and not buy bottle after bottle of some solution that will do little good other than waste your money!

Another of the bigger ripoffs in the building trade is by those who manufacture and market some type of **drain cleaner.** They **just never seem to work** nearly as effectively as a **plunger** and they could harm your pipes. Get that *(good quality)* plunger and be happy.

Q. **I need a new water heater. What do you think about the new SELF-CLEANING water heaters?**

A. Water heaters fill up with all kinds of muck. You see, when you keep hot water contained, it separates the solids, the minerals, and leaves deposits. This residue builds up in the bottom of a water heater.

Self-cleaning water heaters **stir** this stuff up so it runs **through your pipes, through your faucet** and into **your sink**. The name of this particular type of water heater tells what it does - it cleans your **water heater!** Personally, I'd rather leave that gunk and muck and sludge in my **water heater,** wouldn't you? Have you ever **seen** the bottom of a water heater? **Nasty friends, nasty!**

When this **self-cleaning heater** stirs the garbage and *crappola* in the heater and sends this stuff through your pipes, it destroys the washers in your fixtures, clogs up the aerators, and eventually causes you a whole bunch of problems. I think the best place for this muck is where it is now, **in the heater!** Your heater is not made to last a lifetime so, in 10 or 12 years, toss it and buy a new one.

No! I don't recommend self-cleaning water heaters. If you want to clean your present one, do it twice a year. Here's how. On top of your water heater on the cold pipe, there is a valve that shuts the water off **to** the heater. Then, connect a garden hose to the faucet on the heater, turn the heat down to very low on the gas water heater *(or cut off the breaker on the electric water heater)* and open the faucet for it to drain. Make certain your garden hose is long enough so it drains in your flower beds, ditch, etc. After it's drained and clean, disconnect the garden hose, close the faucet and open the supply faucet at the top. Turn your heat back on and it's done!

Please, don't **ever** cook with or **drink** water from the **hot** water faucet. If you ever saw what was in the water heater after 5 or 6 years you'd understand what I'm saying. It is **horrible!** Hot water is for cleaning and bathing only, **not** for human consumption.

Q. I'm a do-it-yourselfer, but the job I'm doing now is trying to replace the leaky faucet on the kitchen sink, but I can not figure out how to get a wrench up *behind* the sink to loosen the #*%&@%* nuts on the old faucet. Is there a trick to doing this?

A.   There **is** a **trick** to most things, and the trick is called **experience.** In this case it's the **tool,** and one only plumbers know about. In fact, they joke about it being "*The only tool on the job-site that nobody ever steals,*" mainly because nobody knows **what** it is or **what** it's for. It's called a **basin wrench** and is the oddest-looking thing you ever saw, and sells for about ten dollars. It will do the job. You can find it at plumbing supply houses and at hardware stores that carry a sizable inventory of plumbing supplies.

Q.   **I need to replace my toilet. But, the nuts that hold the base won't come loose, they just spin. How do I get them off?**

A.   I love these questions because they are simple and I hear them all the time and I know you can drive yourself crazy if you don't know the tricks. The answer is . . . **you can't!** These nuts simply **never** loosen. By the time you need to replace your toilet, these nuts are corroded and just spin. The best way, I've found, is to take a hacksaw blade - just the blade - hold the top of the threads with pliers, stick the blade underneath between the nut and the toilet . . . and **cut** through the bolt as far as you can then snap it with the pliers.

When you get the new toilet, spend five bucks for a new bolt kit that comes with nuts, covers, etc. So you see, you're not a idiot and you **cannot** loosen these things. I recommend you **nuke 'em with that hack saw** and get new ones when you replace the commode.

I use the word "toilet" for simplicity and clarity. I know it's called a *John, commode* and *water closet* as well as a few other expressions I dare not use in this text. *"Think I ain't got **no learnin'**? I are a **colidge graduit!**"*

Q. **All the books I read tell me to place the WAX RING on the toilet before I put it in place. When I try, it keeps falling off before I can set the toilet down. What am I doing wrong?**

A. You know what you're doing wrong? You're reading those dumb books. I can't imagine why, but it seems that **all** the books say that *(except this one)* and there is not a plumber in the world who does it that way.

Put those books away and put the wax ring on the **flange** on the floor. The wax ring is molded bee's wax that will seal the joint between the toilet and the flange, not unlike a gasket on an engine. Then, you take the bolts on either side and put a little of that wax around the bolts so they sit up nice and straight and make sure the **rounded** side of the wax ring is up and the flat side down.

Caution, some wax rings have a poly insert. **Don't** use those because what they do is take a 4-inch or a 3-inch drain and put it down to a 2-inch drain and you'll have things stopping up on you. Just use a plain wax ring and if you need it to be higher because you're putting in a higher floor, use two wax rings. Once you get it all set, pick the toilet up, line the holes so the bolts come through and *smoosh* it down to the floor. It's as simple as that.

Stop reading those dumb books. Carry **my book** around in your pocket and show it to your friends.

Q. **Should I put a WATER HEATER JACKET on my water heater? Some say *yes* and some say it's a waste of time. What do you say?**

A. I say **Yes, No** and **Maybe!** What we're **really** talking about is an **insulation** jacket. In many cases it works very well. But let's take a few examples.

(1) If you live in a **cold** climate where your water heater is located in an unheated garage or an unheated basement, the answer is **Yes.** This jacket is fine. It will save money and help keep the water hot.

(2) If you're in a **hot** climate, and your water heater is in the attic or garage *(somewhere where it's not in an air conditioned environment)*, **don't** put a jacket on it. If you do, it will sweat between the jacket and the metal tank and actually rust the tank. You don't **need** this jacket in a hot or warm climate. You won't lose any heat through the walls of the water heater because it's already warm **outside.**

(3) If you **do** live in a warm climate but your water heater is in an air conditioned garage, laundry room or basement, the answer is **Maybe!** It is usually **wise** to have a jacket on it because this will prevent heat from the water heater heating some air conditioned space. This makes sense, doesn't it? Just don't let anyone try to **sell** you something that looks fancy that will do you no good, okay?

> Most **new water heaters** are **well insulated** and don't need a jacket.

Now, if you **do** live in an area or environment where you use a jacket, know that there are two **types** of jackets, one for **electric** heaters, and one for **gas** heaters. Make certain you buy the correct one. On gas heaters, *(the one that has a flame)* **never** cover this flame because it **could** start a fire.

Q. It seems no matter how often I replace the FLAPPER in my toilet, the water still wants to leak into the bowl. Do I need a new toilet?

A. I will share yet **another** little secret with you. Even in **new** toilets some of the water seems to *drip, drip, drip* because the flapper isn't closing on the flush valve correctly. Do this:

Turn the water off behind the toilet *(a shiny handle that you'll see in plain view)* and flush your toilet a time or two until the tank is drained. Then, get some **Vaseline Petroleum Jelly** from your medicine cabinet, scoop some on your hand, pick up the flapper and **coat** the bottom of the flapper with the Vaseline with maybe a quarter-inch of this jelly. Then, drop the flapper back down and turn the water on. You might never need to do this again; it lasts a long, long time. It will stop that leak and even after it's on a while, it will continue to seal up those tiny cracks that allow those *drip, drip, drips* to literally drive you mad when you are trying to fall asleep.

Q.   **Every time I connect two water pipes, they always seem to have a small LEAK at the connection. What am I doing wrong?**

A.   You're doing something wrong okay, but don't feel bad; it happens to everyone, including me *(but I won't admit it to anyone but you)*. You're probably not using everything you need to use, but I have a simple suggestion for something that will work.

The best invention since bottle beer or throw-away baby diapers is **Teflon Tape.** It costs maybe a dollar for a small roll. You wrap this tape around the pipe threads **before** you put them together and it seals them securely. You can also use this tape for gas connections. Use it for a shower head, faucet, anything with screw head connections.

Q.   **My plumber says he needs to install BACK FLOW PREVENTERS on my outside HOSE BIBS. Sounds like alien talk. Is he trying to rip me off?**

A.   **No!**   These are important nowadays. If you put a hose in a puddle of water while the hose is on *(let's say you're watering your yard)* and, for some reason, the water supply to your house loses power, this power-loss has a **siphoning effect** and begins to pull water **back** into the system. A **Back Flow Preventer** stops this.

This **Back Flow Preventer** is a slight cost and acts as sort of a reverse demand valve; it only allows water to flow one way - **out!** This could prevent dirty water, grass, ants, bugs, trash, dog poop, etc., from getting into your water lines and clogging your pipes and perhaps, even spreading disease.

> What I try to do on my show is to get people to use the correct terminology. A **Hose Bib** is what most people refer to as a faucet. The outside "faucet" with the threaded end is correctly called a **Hose Bib.**

Q.   **I was told that the PRESSURE RELEASE VALVE on my water heater was faulty. Should I be concerned, because my water is still running and I have no problems at this point?**

A.   Your pressure release valve is **extremely** important. If you build up too much pressure in the water heater, that thing can blow up and be as powerful as **forty sticks of dynamite** going off. This is, of course, the most severe thing that can happen to you, but it **can** happen.

If your water heater is in your attic, the roof could end up falling on your head. If it's in your garage, wave *bye-bye* to your garage, a part of your kitchen and your Mercedes Benz. This is how you can check it. It's a small valve with a spring and it is located either on top of your water heater or on the side. You pull it up and it springs back down. If it's shut and doesn't spring, it's faulty. **Check it at least once a year!** Twice, if you have a spare minute.

This is only about a twelve-dollar and fifty-cent item and what it protects against is if the pressure builds up, it **releases** this pressure. Some people try to save money when installing a new water heater and *chinch* on the pressure release valve. **Don't do it! OK?** When you buy a new heater, also buy a new valve to go along with it.

A faulty **PRESSURE RELEASE VALVE** could cost you lot's of money, perhaps even your **life!** If one goes bad, replace it. It's easy to do.

Q. **Sometimes, when I empty my dishwasher, I find ground up food in the bottom. I always rinse my dishes so where is it coming from?**

A. I **hope** you rinse your dishes. Many people don't, especially if your kids do the dishes. They aren't always aware that the food on them needs scraping off. My guess is that your dishwasher is probably **siphoning** food from your **garbage disposal!** You see, when you drain your dishwasher, it goes through the garbage disposal. Under your sink is a black hose that comes from somewhere out of your cabinet and that is the drain hose from the dishwasher.

Put a small nail at the top of the inside of this cabinet *(you know, somewhere in the back and out of sight)* and tie a piece of string around this hose so that the hose is **higher** than the garbage disposal. If the hose lays on the floor of the cabinet and is not looped up, tie it with string and your problems are over.

Simple, huh? Hope I've saved you money that would otherwise go to a plumber. In reality, even the **plumber** is happy with this advice. They hate going out to repair something that takes a minute because they feel guilty about charging you and if they **do**, you get miffed. And if they **don't**, they've lost time, and their time is money. Do it yourself and everybody's happy.

Q. **I'm concerned about lead in my water. Is lead solder *(pronounced sodder)* still used with copper pipe?**

A. I'd recommend you have your water checked by one of the many water filter companies that would **love** to do that for you, **free!** It's a chance for their salespeople to get inside your house and scare you to absolute **death** with what they show you is actually **in** your water.

If their test for lead is positive, it **could** mean it's from the original supply **lines** that **lead** *(pronounced leed)* to your system. In the past, various water districts laid pipes that were put together with lead joints. It isn't **much** lead, only a minuscule amount.

The **solution** I suggest is that you **run your water** for a minute **before** you attempt to drink it or cook with it. This cleans out the lead content. Or, buy a **filter.** You'd think, that over a period of time, these lead tracings would dissipate but for some reason or other, a test will reveal that there is **still** a trace of lead after as long as 20 years. You can bathe in it, wash dishes or clothes with it but it's smart not to **ingest** it!

Copper pipes in older homes were joined together by using lead solder. If water lingers in pipes all night long, some lead will leach into the water. Run the water a bit and then test it. There will not be any traces of lead. Because of this lead problem, manufacturers do not even **make** lead solder any longer. Plumbers are using **silver** solder. This works well and there is no danger. The copper is no trouble and frankly, it is the best type of pipe *(galvanized and PVC are the other types)* to use. Copper is by far the most durable.

If you have these older lines and the lead test shows positive, make certain to run the water for a minute as I recommended, or buy a filter, **especially** if you have young children. But by all means, **don't** drink it without taking these precautions. Lastly, you may buy bottled water.

CHAPTER FIVE

Electrical

Q. **I was just told that I have ALUMINUM WIRING in my house. Do I need to have it completely rewired with COPPER wire?**

A. **Only** if you just hit the lottery and have nothing better to do with your money or you need the write-off. However, I don't like aluminum wire; I like copper wire much better. Do **not listen** to anyone who suggests you need your **entire house rewired** to get rid of the aluminum wiring. Let's get to the heart of the problem.

In the early nineteen seventies, copper got too expensive, so the country went to aluminum wiring, which is **very safe** if used properly. When aluminum wire was first introduced many electricians did not **know** how to install it or they didn't follow the necessary safety standards. But, it's nothing to panic over and the problems are easy to solve.

For instance, at the screw connections on your light switch, when the aluminum wire was screwed down, it was either not tightened securely or the improper switch was used. For aluminum wiring you need receptacles that are rated **CO/ALR**. Most electricians used these **CO/ALR** switches, but some did not.

Many homeowners who have aluminum wiring aren't even aware of it. The first sign of trouble is when they feel their light switch-plate getting warm. The thing to do is **immediately** take off your switch-plate *(that covering over your switch)* and check to see two things:

(a) Make certain that the wires are **tight** around the little screws. If they aren't, it tends to spark, thus heating your switch-plate.

(b) Check to see if the electrician put the aluminum ends in those holes in the back of switch-plates. When these aluminum wires are activated, they heat and **expand** when they are turned on, and then **shrink** when they are turned off and cooled. When this happens, of course the connection becomes loose.

While you have this switch-cover off, take the other two little screws out that fasten the switch to the box, *(there's extra wire to pull it out a bit)* and pull the switch out a few inches and see if it is marked **CO/ALR.** Now, **before** you start messing around with hot wires, make **certain** you have your electricity turned **off. . . from the fuse box!** It's a pain in the neck to do this, but far better than the alternative.

The place where they had the **most** trouble with overheating was at the **refrigerator connection** because it has a motor-load and it heats up fast. Check that receptacle, and make certain it too says **CO/ALR** and that it is screwed on tight.

No! You do **not** need to rewire your entire house with copper wiring, and don't let anyone **install** aluminum wiring while replacing old wire, or if you are building a new house. If you presently have aluminum wire in your home, I want you to feel safe now that it's all been figured out, taken care of, and explained. Just check the "problem areas" I told you about and if you tend to these minor problems quickly and with a degree of intelligence, you'll never have to fear for your safety.

Q. I want to change some lighting fixtures in my house. Do I need an electrician to do this?

A. No, you do **not need an electrician** to change lighting fixtures. Electrical systems in homes are extremely simple, especially general lighting. You must **still** follow a certain procedure to insure your safety. I hate to get trite, but "It's better to be safe, than sorry."

First, turn the power **off** to the lights simply by turning off the switch to that particular light. Then, remove the cover to the fixture, unloosen the bolt that holds it up and look at the wires. White wire to white wire, black wire to black wire and the green is the ground wire. The black wire is the **hot** wire, white is the neutral.

It's easy enough to do, just make certain you turn the power **off** and match the color wires on the new fixture. Then, tighten it up and turn the switch back on and *presto!* You're an electrician.

A "bite" from a live wire will rarely **kill** a person but it very well **could** be enough of a "hit" to cause you to lose your balance and break an arm, leg, or neck. It's happened many times to others. **Don't** let it be you! Follow my safety suggestions when fooling around with "live" connections. "It's better . . . I already said that.

Q. **I'm building a new home and my electrician says I can "get by" with a 150-amp service, but he recommends a 200-amp service. This will cost more, right? What do you think?**

A. I think it's extremely wise to go with the **200-amp** service. Here's why. In older homes, they had as little as 60-amp service since there just weren't as many electrical appliances. Today, I would definitely recommend going to a full 200-amp service. Your building code might not require if when you build your house, but as you add a hot tub, outdoor lighting, garden lighting, a fountain, swimming pool, barbecue pit, computers, shop lights, it's **better** to have the larger service.

The breaker box will have to be **sized** differently to accommodate these extra circuits and you'll have to ask for a **larger** wire from the power company. It costs a bit more for this upgraded power now, but far **less** expensive than having to do it later. Imagine having to **tear out everything** you put in and then ask the power company to dig a hole and install a larger wire. Yeah, do it smart and do it now!

I won't always suggest the **least expensive** way to make these various repairs. I will, however, give you the most **economical** as well as the **safest** way!

Q. **I was told I needed a GROUND FAULT CIRCUIT INTERRUPTER installed in my bathrooms. What in the world are these? I'm only building a house, not a space station. Is my contractor trying to squeeze more money from me on something unnecessary?**

A.   **No!** Your builder is right! I talk to a lot of *old timers* who say, *"We went for years and never had 'em. I don't know why you need 'em. I never got electrocuted."* Maybe they were just lucky.

A **Ground Fault Circuit Interrupter** *(referred to in the trade as a GFI)* is nothing other than a receptacle that measures the **input** and the **output** of the power. The power comes in through the black wire and goes out through the white wire back to the box and makes a complete circle. This **GFI** measures what comes in on the black wire and what goes out on the white wire and if there's any difference in it at all, there's a little fuse in it that goes *"pop"* and shuts off the power to that particular circuit.

Let me tell you the best reason I can think of as to why you need a **GFI.** If you're using a hair dryer, electric razor, curling iron or any electrical device *(especially in your bathroom),* and you're around a wet area and you decide to stick your face in water with that razor or dryer still in your hand, **you** become a ground. Which means, instead of the power going **out** the white wire, it goes through **you!** Chances are you'll sizzle and **die!** *(That's the best example I could think of off the top of my head. Good enough though, huh?)*

This, would probably ruin your day. **Yes**, you need 'em, and more than **just in the bathroom!** You need them within **6 feet** of **any** sink, on the outside of the house where you'll be running these hedge clippers, electric weedeaters, blowers, hot tub, etc. You need them in your garage if you have additional lighting, where you use power tools or a heater in winter. They are well worth the few bucks extra. Now that you heard what they **prevent**, don't you agree?

You can put one on a single receptacle and **all** the switches in that circuit will work off of it. Personally, I'd recommend **one in each area** because once in a while it could snap off and if you're in the tub or shower, you'll look silly if caught in your garage naked looking for the reset button when the UPS man or a Girl Scout selling cookies shows up unannounced.

If you'll notice, **I NEVER GIVE PRICES** on the tools or supplies I recommend because prices vary. Take the time and **go to your favorite store,** you know, the one where you feel comfortable that the prices are fair and the service is good, and price them. Look at the specials in the Sunday paper for comparison-pricing.

Q. I want to install some SECURITY LIGHTS around my house. Any tips on this?

A. **Of course!** I'm the house doctor, remember? I answer **all** problems. The biggest mistake most people make is **overkill!** They want big, bright lights shining out into their yard. What this does is create **dark spots** as well as **light spots.** Even amateur criminals know how to use these contrasting areas to conceal their presence. This also tells the criminal that the homeowner doesn't know much about security and makes them an easier target.

When setting out security lights, think of them as cat's eyes. You want your lighting to be **even** and **consistent**, so you can notice motion and your eyes don't have to continuously adjust to bright, dark, bright, dark etc. An easy test is to install **moderate** lighting and walk around the house testing for dark or light spots to add or take away lights. Then, adjust the direction of the lights accordingly.

If the crooks know that **you** know, they'll pass you by and go to your neighbors house. So, when you're finished with my book, tell your neighbor to buy one too. Don't lend it, because statistics say that loaned books make it back to the original owner only **1** out of **20** times. Besides, I need the money. I've got to make repairs on **my** house too.

Q. I want to replace a light with a ceiling fan. Can I hang the fan from the electrical box?

A.   Perhaps!   But **only** if that box is attached to the **frame.** If not, the fan and light could fall on your head. I knew of one family who didn't check, and they didn't get hurt but their dog, sleeping under it, was **bombed!**

Ceiling fans are **heavy**, and heavier still when you add a light kit. There's a lot of torque being produced when they're spinning and especially when they are on *high.* It's smart to have them secured to the framing. In fact, the *National Electrical Code* on new homes does not **allow** you to hang ceiling fans from the box alone.

For older homes, there's a neat little gadget available now and called an **Easy Fan Brace**. Go to your home improvement store and you'll see what I mean. In fact, why not spend a rainy afternoon *(with my book in one hand)* **at** the home improvement center and look at these various things. Look at them, ask about them, price them, touch them, look at them again and know what you're doing. It could save a lot of money, grief and maybe even your dog's life. Men, take your wives with you and show off. Ladies, since most of you already know a lot about this stuff, **pretend** you don't; this kind of *malarkey* still makes most men happy. Or, **you** show off!

Your fan uses about the same amount of electricity as a 100-watt light bulb. In each fan kit is a wiring diagram; black to black, white to white, green to green and you're in business. If you're not certain, call the person back at the home improvement center and get a telephone explanation.

Q. **When I replace a light fixture, do I have to turn the power** *off* **at the breaker box?**

A. You **could**, but **why?** It is a royal pain in the neck, to put it mildly. First, if your various area fuses aren't marked, you might have to turn power off to the **entire** house before you find the correct one. If it's at night, you might have to work with a flashlight under your chin that could be cumbersome. And if it's day **or** night, you will have to go around and reset **each** clock, the microwave, and don't forget the clock on the VCR; I don't want you taping the wrong programs.

So, the answer to your question is **No.** Just turn the light **switch** *off!* You have now virtually cut the power **off** to that switch and there is no danger of being "bitten" by a hot wire. The overcautious will advise you not to do that and to go to your main fuse box because, "*Somebody will turn the switch on by mistake while you're working.*" This could be true, especially if it's a child tall enough to reach the switch or someone who just came home. But this is easy to remedy.

When you turn the switch *off*, put a piece of electrical tape **over** the switch to make it clear to everyone in the house that you are working in this particular area. If you've just had a heated argument with your wife and she recently upped the amount of your life insurance policy, either wait until everyone is gone, turn the power off at the breaker, get a new wife or **call an electrician!**

CAUTION! If you're working on a light fixture or ceiling fan, the *on/off* switch is all you need be concerned with, you know, the one to that particular fixture. If you want to replace a **receptacle** *(the two little face-like plugs in your wall)* and you're working with wires that you can't identify, **especially 220 volt wiring,** *(washer, dryer, AC system, maybe hot tub, swimming pool)* turn **off** the power at the fuse box! I recommend that you do bear the inconvenience of resetting your various appliances or chance feeling as if you were hit by a bolt of lightning.

Q. **I have a fluorescent light that keeps flickering. I replaced the bulbs but it still jumps. What else can I do to find out what's wrong?**

A. Fluorescent lights have three major parts, the **bulb,** the **starter** and the **ballast.** After you're tried putting in new bulbs without success, in most cases it's cheaper to just replace the **entire fixture! Compare** the cost of replacing the ballast, the starter or the complete fixture. Be a *smart, stopper.* I mean a *short, snapper.* I mean a **smart shopper!** But always start with replacing the bulb. If this isn't the problem, you have replacement bulbs for your new fixture.

Q. **I notice that the light switch on my wall feels warm after its been on for a while. Do I have a problem? Should I call an electrician?**

A. **Yes!** You do have a problem, but **No,** it isn't necessary to call an electrician at this point. Do this. Turn the power *off* to it, from the **fuse box!** Then, take off your switch-plate, pull the switch out *(wires are long enough for you to pull it out a little so you can see)* and I'll bet you have a loose connection. Chances are that's all that is wrong with it. Simply tighten down the screws and you're back in business. When the wires aren't tight, it could produce sparks, therefore it heats up and could be dangerous. Do **not** let this receptacle go unattended. It's too easy to fix. If it **still** gets warm after you've tightened these wires, **then** call the electrician.

This last problem is similar to the home where the person had **aluminum** wire. But, if **any** connection is loose *(even a copper wire connection)* it produces sparks and could warm the cover plate. Tighten the connection and everything should be fine.

Q. **I have a LIGHT DIMMER-SWITCH. Can I use it to regulate my ceiling fan speed?**

A. **No!** A dimmer-switch is what we call a **rheostat** and there are various kinds of these switches; most are made for dimming lights and **some** are made for fans. Do **not** use a light dimmer-switch *(rheostat)* for a ceiling fan. Get the one that is made **exclusively** for ceiling fans.

CHAPTER SIX

Painting & Wallpapering

Q. I have old, dark paneling in my kitchen and family room. I'd like to lighten it up. Should I just paint it or can I do something else with it?

A. The only way to lighten it **without** painting it is to **tear it out and replace it** or **sheetrock over the top of it!** If you're thinking of changing the color by staining or white-washing it, it is difficult to do. The most economical way to lighten it **is** to paint it. It's the trend now to **paint over** tired, old colors. Here's how I recommend you do it.

Do **not** sand it! This is one of the first mistakes most people make. It is a **veneer,** and when you sand through the top of veneer you make a huge mess that really isn't necessary. Instead, use a **liquid deglosser** and wipe it down. Then, use an **interior, oil-based primer.** This **seals in** the dark wood so it doesn't bleed through your final coat of paint.

After you prime it, **caulk** all the joints with an **acrylic latex with silicone.** The joints I'm referring to are between the paneling; where the baseboard meets the paneling and where the window trim and door trim meets the paneling because you'll have dark lines that need to be caulked.

Once you caulk it, I recommend **two** coats of **interior oil-base trim paint.** Please, don't try using only **one** coat. It won't look the same. Do it right **this time** and you won't have to do it over again. Another big mistake is in trying to use a **latex** paint, and latex on woodwork does **not** mix.

Q. I just added a room to my house and now it's time to paint the inside. Should I use a different type of paint on woodwork than I do on the sheetrock?

A. Yes! There are more tricks to try, so let's start with the sheetrock. If you choose a **flat** paint on the sheetrock, go ahead with **two** coats of **flat latex** *(a water based paint).* If you want a **sheen** or **finish** like an eggshell, satin or semi-gloss look, you have to **seal** the sheetrock first with a **sheetrock primer** and then apply the semi-gloss or satin paint. These will **still** be **water-based latex** paints.

For woodwork on the **inside** of the house, **always** use an **oil-based** paint! The new word recently adopted by the painting world is **solvent-based** paint. It gives a harder finish, and won't chip or peel like the latex will on the woodwork. On the inside, always use an **interior, oil-based trim paint** on all doors, the woodwork, cabinets or paneling.

Q. I painted the exterior of my house about 6 months ago and the paint looks fine, but knotholes are bleeding through and they look awful. What can I do to cover these blemishes?

A. This is not uncommon. Tannic acids want to bleed through any of the paints. Here's my recommendation for cover those knotholes or stains.

Paint over those problem areas with **Pigmented Shellac.** Then, touch up the spots with some of the leftover paint I know you were wise enough to keep when you originally painted your house, weren't you? This should solve that problem.

On **new** wood, use an **exterior oil-based primer** and then a **latex** final coat. The *(EPA) Environmental Protection Agency* has regulated the painting industry so stringently that the "good stuff" that used to be in the **exterior oil-based paint** is just not there anymore, and this new stuff doesn't hold up to the weather. Use the primer and **then** apply your latex final coat. Six months down the line, **if** the knotholes show bleeding or if stains reappear, go back around with the pigmented shellac.

Q. **I am going to repaint the exterior of my house, but I must first replace some pine siding. Any tips?**

A. **Before** you put pine siding on a house, to make it stable, to keep it from wanting to twist or crack or cup, **prime** the back. Then, prime the front and paint it. What this back and front primer will do is allow it to dry out evenly so it doesn't want to cup to the outside or inside and it will hold better. I'll tell you why we have this problem.

The **trees** we are now using to get this pine come from **tree farms.** There are no longer "old" trees they were pulling straight out of the forest four or so decades ago, the ones with the real tight grains. These new "farm-trees" are usually young and the grains are open and, regardless of the grade you buy, the wood is generally unstable. But, you can overcome this by priming it, causing it to become more stable, and last a lot longer.

Q. **I just built a new home and used Red Western Cedar Siding. I really like the rough, textured look but I'd like to paint it a solid color. What is the proper procedure?**

A. A lot of people think you **can't** paint cedar and some people can't stand to **see** it painted for the mere fact that it's so pretty and that when you paint it, you cover the natural beauty. Cedar **is** beautiful when first put on a home, but to **keep** it looking fresh and new is impossible. You'll have to, eventually, stain it or paint it. There are two ways to approach it. One, is with a **solid color stain**, which is my preference, because it penetrates. It is a **linseed oil-based** stain with **solid pigment** so it gives you the **colors** of paint *(white, red, the natural wood colors, etc.)* but by penetrating, you won't get **peeling** problems.

If you really want a **hard paint finish,** you can do it by applying a good coat of **oil based primer** *(keeps the tannic acids from coming through)* and then, of course, a couple of coats of **good** latex.

There are **good paints** and there are **crummy paints.** I truly want to save you money, but by **"chinching"** on paint **is not the way!** I prefer the brand-name paints that have solid back-up warranties.

Q. **I just built some play equipment for my children using pressure-treated pine. I am getting several conflicting reports on painting it. Let's hear your suggestion on this.**

A. If it's **kiln dried** like it's supposed to be, you can paint it anytime you want. If it's real wet, let it dry out a while before you attempt to paint it, and paint it just like you'd paint any other wood; use the **oil-based exterior primer,** use that **pigmented shellac** for knotholes and stains, and finish up with a **latex** final coat. Use two coats to do it right.

Q. **I had a roof leak, and it resulted in some large water-stains on my ceiling sheetrock. I painted over these stains after the sheetrock dried, but the stains came back. Do I have to replace the whole panel of sheetrock?**

A. **No, you don't!** Water stains will **continue** appearing if you don't **seal them in!** When the area dries, seal it with that **pigmented shellac** I mentioned earlier. Most people think shellac comes in a clear color and it does, but this pigmented type has a tinge of white and will cover your stain. Then, paint your ceiling any color you choose.

If you **begin** by doing these things **correctly,** or by **repairing** them correctly, chances are you won't have to do them **again** for a very long time, maybe ever!

Q. **I have wallpaper that just doesn't want to come off the wall. Can I just paint over it, or put new wallpaper over it?**

A. Believe it or not, you **can** just leave it there! You can either paint over **or** wallpaper over it. **But,** guess what you must use to seal it in? You're right. **Pigmented Shellac!** What it will do is **seal in** the old wallpaper pattern because patterns will bleed though paint and sometimes it will even bleed right through the new wallpaper.

If you want to change the **look** on this wall *(join the club),* you can put on **joint-compound texture,** then either splatter or roll on the new texture, and then paint it your new chosen color. To put new **wallpaper** over it, use the pigmented shellac. Then, when it dries put sizing on it, and paper right over it.

This can be done **only** if it's "real" wallpaper. If it's **Mylar** or a **foil**, it **must come off!** How do you remove these coverings? Your answer is two questions down.

Q. **I'm about to try wallpapering a wall that is now painted. The wall is smooth. Do I still need to use SIZING before I paper it? If so, why?**

A.   **Sizing**, will make your life easier "down the road." It helps the glues to adhere better and faster. It helps the wallpaper to stick when you first put it on, and when the time comes to **take that paper off** *(maybe **you**, and if not, **somebody** will want to eventually),* it makes it easier. Besides, sizing is easy to apply so spend the extra bucks and do it right.

Q. **As I was removing some old wallpaper from my sheetrock, I had to rip some of the paper off and it left rough spots and sometimes big gouges in the sheetrock. What do I do now?**

A.   In **removing** old wallpaper, assuming the surface wasn't prepared properly, *(no **sizing**)* you **will** have some problems. To **remove it**, either rent a **steamer** or buy **chemical strippers**. These will make the wallpaper easier to **remove** but, chances are high that it will **still score**, and sometimes even **gouge** chunks from the sheetrock. Here's how you handle these problems.

     After the paper is off and you have these holes and pock marks, I suggest you use **joint compound** and a big sheetrock knife and **float over it.** Did you do something wrong? Not at all, except maybe start doing this work yourself. There are **some** jobs where it's best to call in a professional! Wallpapering, though easy, **can** be a major headache and if you have a fine home, unless you're a near-expert at wallpapering, call in a *pro*.

Q. **I'd like to paint the brick on my house. Can I do it and if so, how do I go about doing it?**

A. **Absolutely!** But, **before** you start painting, mix a solution of half-water\half-bleach and with an ordinary garden sprayer, spray it on to **clean off** any mold and mildew. Then, hose it off. And **then,** paint it with a **Masonry Primer** to make your paint hold better. Finish up with a coat a **good quality latex** paint. It will make your home look new and beautiful.

If you want to paint **inside** brick, like around your fireplace or maybe a brick wall, just vacuum-brush it and paint over it with a **semi-gloss latex paint.**

> Just remember this! Once you paint brick, it is there **forever!** The only way to get paint off of bricks, is to sandblast, and this is a difficult, expensive, exhausting measure. To get paint off a few bricks, use sandpaper.

Q. **We had a small fire in the kitchen. The walls and cabinets have smoke stains that won't wash off. Can I paint over the damaged areas, or do I have to buy new cabinets?**

A.   For the first part of your question, the answer is **Yes!** Professionals in smoke restoration will not even **attempt** washing the stains off because most will not come off. They **do,** however, paint **over** the stains with **Aluminum** paint! You can do the same.

This aluminum paint is marvelous. It seals in **the smell, the smoke stain, the fire stain, everything!** Many homes that have had large fires where the rafters are still good, the *pros* will go into the attic and spray everything with this aluminum paint and save a lot of money.

Thus, you already have the answer to your second question, **No!** There is no need to replace cabinets. Just paint over them **after** you first use this aluminum paint.

Did you think they didn't **have** this type of paint for smoke and fire damage? Come on now. We put a man on the **moon,** for goodness sakes. Surely there is something to handle **whatever** happens to your home. The "good old days" certainly have merit, but I truly appreciate modern technology in home repairs.

CHAPTER SEVEN

Ceramic Tile

Q. I am in the midst of remodeling my bathroom and it has become a major undertaking. I plan to tile the floor and shower. What type of adhesive should I use to set the tile?

A. There are two major types of adhesives, **Thin-Set** adhesives and **Mastic-Set** adhesives.

(1) The **Thin-Set Adhesive** mixes with water. It's a portland or masonry product, and used mainly for **floors.** There are two **types** of thin-set adhesive. One is the **plain-set** adhesive and the other is called **multi-purpose.**

If you're laying tile on the **outside** of the house, use the **plain thin-set.** It's slower curing and doesn't react to movement as well as the other type, but it reacts to the weather changes better.

For **inside** tile, you'll want to use a **multi-purpose thin-set.** The benefit of this type is that it has a **latex additive** so if there is any movement of your slab, or if your floors move a little bit, if there's grease or paint on the floor, *(floors don't have to be **perfectly** clean for this type)* it will hold much better.

(2) The **Mastic Adhesive** is pre-mixed in paste form. **Use** this **Mastic Adhesive** on the **walls** and **ceilings**, such as in the shower and tub. This **pre-mixed** mastic makes the tile stick right to the walls as well as to just about any kind of surface.

Q. I went to the home improvement store to buy GROUT for my tile job. It was recommended that I buy a LATEX ADDITIVE to make the grout a bit stronger. Is this necessary?

A. I try to **discourage** most do-it-yourselfers from using a latex additive. It **does**, in fact, make the grout stronger. **But**, if you don't mix the batches **exactly right,** you'll experience color changes. If you buy colored grout as most people do *(as opposed to the plain white type)* and if the additive isn't mixed **just right**, sometimes a milky haze bleeds through. So, it's **your** choice. An additive will make it **stronger,** but it could also make it **ugly!**

If you mix your grout properly with just water, it will be **plenty strong enough** for you and there is no need to buy and add these latex additives.

I don't recommend people using the **Latex Additives** unless they are very, **very** experienced with it. Maybe try some on a **neighbor's** tile first.

Q. **There are so many different types of grout on the market, how do I know which to buy?**

A.   Color-matching grout will make tile floors look either really good or if the color is wrong, they will look "funny" forever. Grout is the part that people complain about most, because it gets dirty so easily. The two general types are a **sanded** grout and one **without** sand.

   (1) NON-sanded grout goes in a joint **LESS** than one eighth of an inch wide.

   (2) SANDED grout is for joints an eight of an inch wide or wider! The sand serves as a filler. I refer to it as an "aggregate."

   There is a **third** type of grout called an **Epoxy Grout** that is more difficult to use and is mostly for areas where you might experience chemical-spills such as in a dark room, or where you might use chemicals to clean things.

Q. **I just finished tiling my kitchen and it came out great. I'd like to keep it looking new. What can I use on it?**

A.   We're back to the **grout** again, and the grout gets dirty. As far as tile, especially if it's a good grade of tile, the only thing you need to keep it clean is water. It has the same type ceramic glaze on it as a **dish.**

What you **need to do** is to **seal** the grout! Buy a **silicone grout sealer**, pour it over the grout and tile, wipe it with a sponge over the tile and grout, and the grout will absorb this sealer. Let it set for a while and dry, then wipe it with a towel. You can buff it off the tile but it **soaks** down into the grout. You will probably have to do this several times *(until the grout won't absorb any more).*

If you have the time and the patience, I'll share a little trick with you that will do it right the **very first time** around and your grout will stay clean and look wonderful forever.

Take some **Clear Lacquer,** and with a tiny paint brush, paint the **top of the grout joints.** Once you do this, it is sealed **forever!** With the **silicone sealer** I first mentioned, it will **look** great for a while, but in maybe 6 months it has to be done again. With the **lacquer,** if you will take the time, it will **always** look fresh and clean. Just wipe it with water, same as your tile.

Q. **My house was only 3 years old when the tile in the shower fell off the wall! It seems the sheetrock it was attached to just crumbled away. Was this installed properly?**

A. **No, it wasn't!** In tubs and showers - wet areas - one of the most **misused** products is something called **Green Rock** or **Blue Board.** This is a water **resistant** sheetrock. It is not water **proof,** and will, over a short period of time, deteriorate.

Grout **is not waterproof either**, and over a period of time, water **will** seep through the grout. When water gets **behind** this grout *(and it will)*, it starts to tear away at the sheetrock and water **resistant** material cannot take a steady diet of being rained or showered upon. No matter how good your tile is or how well your glue was applied, when the backing crumbles, you have to tear **everything** out and start all over again.

On your **new** tub or shower area, use **Backer Boards**. These are half-inch-thick concrete boards that are nailed to the framing and are water**proof**. They have a fiberglass mesh on the outside and masonry on the inside *(a Portland product)* and purportedly lasts forever!

In the "old" days, we had to put a **wire mesh** on the walls, **pack it** with three layers of our own mortar mix, and **stick on** the tiles. This was called **thick-set**.

Q. I want to tile my kitchen countertop and back-splash. I now have some type of plastic laminate *(formica)* on the countertop. Do I have to remove this covering before I install tile?

A. 'Fraid so! You **cannot** install tile on plastic laminate. Some try to use a belt sander and rough up this Formica and hope the glue will stick the tiles to it - and it **will!** But remember, this plastic laminate is nothing more than **compressed paper** with a plastic on top. If you rough it up, sand it, or take the plastic off, you'll be gluing mostly to **paper!** This is **not** my favorite backing material for tile. Once water leaks through, **and it will,** the tiles come up.

But, here's another of my **tricks.** Buy quarter-inch-thick concrete *(or half-inch-thick)* **Backer Board** and **nail** it right on the top of your Formica. This gives you a hard, waterproof surface with which to glue your tile. Be **careful** when you remove the edging. You can take this off by sticking a putty knife behind one corner and spray **lacquer thinner** behind it. The glue will loosen, and the Formica comes right off.

You **will** have to pull your sink or cook-top up because that will have to be reset again, but that has to be done regardless of what you do to the countertop.

Q. I have a bathroom with a vinyl floor over a wood subfloor and the vinyl seems to be glued down well. Can I lay ceramic tile over this or does the vinyl have to be removed?

A. I would **never** lay any type of tile over a wood sub-floor, whether the vinyl is flat and well fastened or not. Vinyl **isn't** the issue; the wood floor **is!**

Again, the **remedy** is **concrete Backer Board!** You can put it over the vinyl and then add tile to it. In doing this, there are a few steps. First, you put on a layer of **thin-set adhesive** on the vinyl, put the backer board on top, and nail **through** the vinyl and **into** the wood subfloor. When that sets, put **another** layer of **thin-set adhesive** on **top** of the backer board and lay your tile.

If you have a vinyl floor on a **concrete** slab, or a **concrete** subfloor, and the vinyl is old, there is a product for this called a **primer** that you paint on the vinyl, let it dry, then use the **thin-set adhesive on that,** and it works well.

> When you tile over this vinyl and the additional **height** to your flooring is a problem, **cut your bathroom door to fit** and *(of course)* reset your toilet.

Q. **My tub-surround was just installed 6 months ago. It consists of ceramic tile, but all the grout seems to be crumbling out of the corners. What can I do?**

A. One of the **biggest mistakes** a tile man can make is to **grout** the areas where the walls meet the walls, and the walls meet the tub. You're not **supposed** to grout that because when the house moves *(all houses move)* the grout will chip out and water gets behind it to cause problems. Those areas are supposed to be **caulked - not grouted!**

The caulking needs to be an **Acrylic Latex with Silicone.** This makes it **flexible** and it can handle the movement. It's chemical makeup is such that it won't crack or crumble and come out of the joints.

Q. **The soap dish on my bathtub was accidentally pulled off the wall, but it's not broken. How can I attach it back to the wall?**

A. The soap dish usually has a "handle-looking" piece on it, but these would-be handles were not meant to be **grabbed** on. Those handles, believe it or not, were made to drape your wash cloths over to dry. But, you pulled it off or it fell off and attaching it back is fairly simple.

Use a **Construction Adhesive!** Most people call it by the brand name, *Liquid Nails.* It comes in a caulk tube, usually brown in color. Just *goop* it all over the back of the fixture, stick the fixture back on the wall and prop it up the best you can with tape, a broom, or anything to hold the fixture in place to give it time to dry. Then caulk it where it meets the tile and it's there forever.

The next time you get out of the tub and want a "grabber", install a bar or handle on the wall and attach it **to the framing.** If you grab the soap dish handle again, chances are the **dish** won't come off *(it might break)* but you'll pull your **wall off** the studs because that adhesive really holds.

You have but **one chance** to make certain the re-stuck soap dish is straight. If it's not, you had best learn to live with it; once it's fastened with this adhesive, you can't blast it off with dynamite!

Q.   **My shower is tiled, but the ceiling is painted. I have some extra tiles and would like to tile the ceiling too. But, the grout joints will not line up with all four walls. It looks impossible to match them. Do you have a trick to do this?**

A.   **Of course I do!** And, it **is** impossible to match them, unless you try this. Take the ceiling tiles and turn them on a **45-degree angle.** This way they'll **never** meet and it looks as if it was done on purpose.

The "tile guys" know it's impossible to line these tiles where they look even, and that's why **they** always do it this way. Just mark off your lines at a 45-degree angle from corner to corner, stick up your mastic, and start tiling. It should come out looking great. If not, close your eyes when you shower and just don't look at it. Seriously, it will look terrific!

CHAPTER EIGHT

Basic Home Care

Q. **Every fall, my roof gets covered with LEAVES and PINE NEEDLESS. A neighbor told me that this actually PROTECTS the shingles. Is this true?**

A. **Hardly!** The person who told you this is **not** one to advise you on buying stock, either. What these leaves and pine needles do, is **eat** the shingles right off the roof! You need to get those things **off** that roof as fast as you can. Let me give you some choices on how to do this.

I'd try a strong hose and attempt washing them off. Or a strong blower to blow them off. You might have to get **on the roof** and sweep or rake them off but, by all means, **do** get them off! Those dreaded **pine needles** are the worst! The acids from them will literally **destroy** your roof!

Whenever they form a pile, get to them, especially in the areas of the **valleys** because this debris will keep the area **damp**, which cuts down your "roof-life" as much as **twenty-five percent!** Don't listen to your neighbor with this incorrect advice, listen to me.

One of my listeners made a **roof-rake** by using half-inch *PVC* pipe. She compared it to building with *Tinker Toys,* and said it was fun and easy. Her rake was 20 feet long, she put a 45-degree elbow on the handle and the rake part, made with 6 T's of *PVC* with six *PVC* "teeth", could reach far enough up her roof for her to stand on the ground and rake. *PVC* is very inexpensive and it sounds like a fun project.

If a **tree limb** is rubbing on your roof, **cut it down!** It has the same effect as a dozen **NFL lineman** running on it with cleats. When it's windy, the limb will scrape and grind on the granules and **eat a hole** in your roof.

Q. **My wife and I love to use the FIREPLACE in the winter. Is there something I need to do before I start it up again? And maybe something I need to do after using it?**

A.   **Yes,** several things. Maintenance is **always** cheaper and far safer. First, it's wise to have the chimney **swept** at least once a year by a professional to get the creosote out of the flue. Creosote is simply unburned wood that goes up the chimney and sticks to the sides, and if enough has gathered on the walls, it **can** start a fire. Also check for birds or bird nests and clean those out too.

Check those **Fire Bricks** by making certain the mortar *(or fire clay)* between them is in good shape. You can purchase a tube of **fire clay** in a caulk tube from just about any home improvement center or hardware store for around three bucks to **fill up those gaps.**

Make certain your **damper** is working properly, that it opens and closes as it should, and that it's clean. You can do this on your own or, when you have the chimney swept, they will do this automatically.

It's also smart to have a **cap** on your fireplace to keep the weather and birds *(including bird **droppings**)* from getting in. Fireplaces are great, but they need maintenance. Each large city has a *Chimney Sweep Guild*, probably listed in your *Yellow Pages.* Call for prices.

Q. **I have OIL STAINS ON MY DRIVEWAY. What can I use to remove them?**

A. Wherever you drive or park your car, you'll eventually have oil stains. That's just the way it is. And the oil stains get down in that porous concrete and make your floor look absolutely filthy. **But**, there are some **tricks** to getting these stains removed.

Get some **Mineral Spirits** and pour it over the stained area. Then, take some **clay cat litter** and scatter that over the top of the stain. Then get a **brick**, and with the smooth side of the brick, **grind** the cat litter into the mineral spirits. Let it set overnight then sweep it up.

If there's a lot of oil, you'll have to do this several times. Chances are, if these oil stains are old, you'll **never** get them **all** up but you'll clean a large amount of it. If you get the stain while it's reasonably fresh, you might get it all.

Q.   **I just put a new counter top in my kitchen and the island portion is a large butcher block made of solid wood. What can I use to seal it?**

A.   **Never** put a sealer of any type on a butcher block **if** you use it to **prepare food!** If you want to bring some life back to that block, use **mineral oil (only)** and rub it in with a rag, let it dry overnight, then wipe off any excess.

If the butcher block is **not** going to be used for preparing food, you can paint it with **Poly Urethane** that will protect it against spills and stains. If it is to be used only to **look at** and you need to get it clean, **sand** it and then put your coating on it.

Q.   **I've lived in my house for about 10 years and never gave termites a thought. But my neighbor just had an inspection done and they found termites. Is it time to panic?**

A.   **Why panic?** It won't solve a thing. Either you have them and you do something about it, or you don't have them. Make an inspection on your own by walking around your house at least once a year. If your house is on a concrete slab, it's relatively easy. But here is the termite schedule and some of their habits.

Each **Spring,** termites swarm and drop their wings everywhere. They start to move, and hunt for a place to retire. And, they might choose **your** home. Just walk around your house looking at the ground and your slab to see if you see any termite **mounds** coming up into your house or little piles of sawdust and/or dirt mounds. Termites cannot live outside, so they construct this mound to protect themselves. They then get into the wood which also protects them. When you see wood with the inside eaten away, it is **severe.** Call the termite people.

Inside your home, look underneath your kitchen cabinets where your plumbing comes through. You can also see them (if they're there) by opening the small trap door behind your bathtub. These areas are susceptible to termite infestation. Look for those trails that lead to wood. If you see a mound going up a drain pipe and it seems vacated, it is! The chief termite made an error and they will continue their search for **wood** to start a new mound.

If your house is on **blocks,** crawl around under it with a flashlight, and look closely at the perimeter walls and interior piers for their telltale mounds. If you see **any** signs of this at all, it's time to call in your termite man.

Q. **The grills on my air conditioning ducts have black mildew on them. Is something wrong with my air conditioning system?**

A. What everybody calls "grills" are really called **registers.** And these registers, probably made of metal, will get moldy and mildewy. What happens is they get very cold when the air conditioner is running, and then the AC shuts off and it warms. When the hot humid air rises and touches it, it reaches dew point, and sweats. This is when mold and mildew appear.

There's nothing wrong with your system other than, during spring cleaning each year, the registers *(grills)* should be taken down, cleaned in the sink with some bleach and water, and re-installed. Of course, very few of us will do that but it's easy and if you don't, dark, mildew-stained vents/grills/**registers** is what you will see.

When taking these registers down, since many are painted in place, there's a little **trick** to doing this correctly. Take a single-edge razor blade or sharp knife and cut around the edge where the paint is sealed so when you do remove this register, you won't take wallpaper or sheetrock **with** it. Cut the seal, unloosen the two screws, put them in your pocket, clean the register, and put it back up.

In fact, if you want to make the job easier for **next year,** throw the metal registers away and purchase the **plastic** type. The plastic doesn't get cold like the metal and therefore, there should be no problem.

Is all this gunk and mildew also in your duct work or air conditioner? **No!** It's happening right there at the surface and you'll even see a bit of it spreading on the sheetrock where the mold and mildew spreads. If you want a **quick fix,** turn your AC system *off* and mix half bleach and half water, put it in a small spray bottle and **mist** the areas that have the black mold and mildew. What it'll do is **kill** the surface mold and mildew and the job is **almost** as thorough as if you took the register **down** to clean it.

Q. **The caulking around my tub is cracking and coming loose. This has happened twice in the past 9 or 10 years. How do I fix it permanently?**

A. This is a **basic** home care problem that happens around your tub, around the base of your commode *(toilet),* and where your kitchen sink meets your countertop, because **caulking**, eventually **wears out.** It's only this **warranty** business again.

You buy these caulk tubes that read, *"Good for 15 years. Good for 25 years, etc."* **Baloney!** Expect about **five** years from caulking before it needs to be redone. Here's how you do it.

Scrape out the old caulk, take some **Mineral Spirits** to wipe the area down, and the mineral spirits *(remember?)* will cause the **new** caulking to **adhere** better. You then caulk it with an **acrylic latex with silicone** and plan to do it again in another five or so years.

Caulk again as soon as your present caulking cracks or separates. If not, water will get behind places where it's not supposed to be and then - major problems!

Q. **When I turn my faucet on in my bathroom sink, water SQUIRTS in all directions. I get more on ME than in the sink. Can you advise me on this?**

A. *"Oh ye of little faith,"* of **course** I can! This is an **easy** one to solve. Just unscrew that little metal mesh on the end of your faucet nozzle; it's called an **Aerator.** If it's too tight to unscrew with your fingers, get a pair of pliers, put a washcloth around the end so you won't scar the pipe, and take it off. It will be filled with all kinds of little rocks and sediment, brought in through the hot water side.

This debris blocks water flow completely, or causes it to squirt in all directions. Just rinse it out with water from the faucet you just took it from, and put it back on. If it's really grungy, go to any hardware or home improvement store and buy a new one for a couple of bucks.

Q. **I have some LOOSE BRICK on my house. What is the best way to remedy this problem without calling over a brick mason?**

A. **Do it yourself,** it's easy. Get a hammer, gently tap to loosen the brick more, and slip it right out of its hole. There's no danger of the other bricks collapsing even if you take three or four of them out. These bricks are mortared together and are quite strong. If it's stuck more firmly than you thought, jiggle it a bit with your fingers and loosen it to pull it out. Then, clean the vacated hole.

Using a small cold chisel or large screwdriver and hammer, chip away the mortar. Then, buy a bag of **mortar-mix** and *slop* some in there. Shove it in with your hand, replace the brick, and smooth the joints with your fingers. It's difficult to make it look too bad. Next, take a wet sponge and wipe the residue *(if any)* off the brick and let it fly. It will look fine.

A **second** choice on filler is to get the kind that comes in a **caulk tube** but frankly, I like the mortar-mix best to repair loose brick. This tube-caulk-mortar-mix *(to me)* looks too much like caulking and **not** mortar.

The **problem** about buying mortar-mix is that you can't buy a "little bag" of it; I think the smallest amount they sell comes in a **forty-pound** bag. Still, it's about the same price as the caulk tube and you have a lot left over to do other things like, if you have **other** loose bricks that will need to be repaired, or brick patios or walkways need patching. Go for the big bag!

Q. **Many of the doors and locks in my house stick and squeak. How can I remedy this problem?**

A. Some people **like** squeaky doors because they can hear their kids come in late. I hate it! If you want to fix this problem, get a can of **Silicone Spray**. It is a terrific **lubricant** for just such a problem. It works in seconds and is inexpensive. You can find it at most hardware stores, even places like *K-Mart* and *Wal*Mart*.

Stick the thin tube that's fastened to the can into the spout of the can, the other into the hard-to-open lock, and give it a squirt. Put your key in the lock and move it back and forth a few times and you'll be **amazed** at the difference. Do the same thing to the door hinges and locks on your car. You can also spray your garage door track, the rollers, hinges, the chain *(if you have an automatic opener)* and **anywhere** metal rubs against metal.

Q.   **The other day, my neighbor's air conditioner DRIP-PAN overflowed into her house. Is there a way I can check mine so this doesn't happen to me?**

A.   **Yes, there is!** And it needs to be done on a regular basis, **especially** during the summer when you use your air conditioner a lot. Most AC's will be in the attic. For those of you who are unaware and/or who have never actually **been** in your attic, you'll see a big monster of a machine.

There are two ends to this machine; the end with the filter is the beginning of the system. At the other end is the evaporator coil *(nothing other than a square little box)* but underneath this box is a **pan**. The pan is visible to you and if you try to find it, you will. If you see **water** in the pan, you have a problem. The pan is there for an **emergency** - in the event your evaporator coil starts to overflow. This is a common problem, and **unless** you have an air conditioner repair person **clean** the evaporator coil on a yearly basis, the chance of it **overflowing** is an ever-present danger.

To **avoid** this problem, go into your attic once a month to inspect this pan. I say this although I'd venture a guess that 99 out of a hundred, **No**, 999 out of a **1000** homeowners **never** do this, as simple as it is to do. It's usually dark in the attic or under this area so bring along a flashlight and if there's water in the pan, call your serviceman. If it's dry, no problem. **But**, to **insure against a problem,** call your air conditioner repair company to have the AC cleaned and serviced on a yearly basis.

You can empty this pan for a temporary fix, but call a repair man because this clogging is indicative of a more **serious** problem. If your evaporator coil caused the drain to clog, it is a warning that your air conditioning system is headed for an expensive overhaul. That's why I emphasize, **maintain** it with a yearly inspection.

> Take a small bucket of water, hold it over your couch or dining room table, and spill it! Quite a **lot** of wetness from it, huh? Just **think** if a pipe in your attic bursts if a cold freeze "happens" when you're away from home on a weekend. Water flows the same as if you turned a faucet on and let it run. I've **seen** it, and the **only** difference between this and a flood is that this water is clean. **Wrap those pipes!**

Q. **It seems that the first time I use my FURNACE in the winter, it stinks up my house. Got a trick to solve this?**

A.   **You bet I do!** It **does** stink up your house too, doesn't it? Try this. When you **know** that winter is coming, **before** the first cold snap hits, you can **open all the windows in your home,** turn the heater up to about 85 degrees, and run that puppy for about 30 minutes. It will burn the dust and **"stuff"** that gathered and settled on your heat exchanger all summer, **de**-stink it, and get the system working clean. With the windows open and ceiling fans on, you can blow that stink outside.

Abraham Lincoln said, *"You can fool **all** of the people **some** of the time; and **some** of the people **all** of the time; but you can't fool **all** of the people **all** of the time."* But, with some of the absurd warranties many of these manufacturers put on their goods, it seems they can fool **enough** of the people **enough** of the time to make a lot of money from their bogus statements.

CHAPTER NINE

Energy Conservation Tips

Q. I always hear about CAULKING windows to save money on my energy bill. Does this *really* have much affect?

A. **It really and truly does!** You can **measure** the effectiveness of these energy conservation tips if you weigh out the effort and expense in **trying** this against paying high energy bills. The caulking is cheap and it's an easy job to caulk your windows. If you're on a fixed income and care about saving money, do it.

The best way to caulk your windows is on the **inside**, where the sheetrock meets the window. Caulking on the **outside** of your house is more for weathering, you know, mostly to keep the rain out.

Q. I just purchased an old house. What's the *first* thing I should do to make it more energy efficient?

A. Depending on how much money you have to spend, there are several things to do. The first thing I recommend is to **make sure you have sufficient attic ventilation!** This means soffit vents all the way under the overhangs and a

continuous ridge vent across the peak of your roof. This give you an incredible amount of savings in several ways:

(1) In the summertime, you'll have a well-vented attic for the heat to get out and this decreases your cooling bill.

(2) It exhausts the heat and the moisture *(moisture being in the wintertime)* and your **paint** stays on the house longer. That's energy savings.

(3) Your **shingles** or other roofing material might last 20 to 30 percent **longer!** I don't think they'll make that 40-year warranty but it will increase their life considerably, maybe 4 to 6 years. This means you save money on more than just your energy bills.

> In the **winter** is when you need this ventilation the most. When moisture builds up because of the heat, it causes your **paint to peel**, your **shingles to curl**, your **roof to deteriorate**, and your **insulation to become less effective**. All of this, costs you money!

Q. **I have recently seen something advertised called a PROGRAMMABLE THERMOSTAT. What is it, will it save me money on my energy bill, and can I install one myself?**

A. **Yes, and Yes.** It all depends on how you **program it.** If you do it the way I tell you, it will save you considerable money. Here are some tips to follow that will make it worth the purchase.

About a half hour **before** you leave your house to go to work, set this **Programmable Thermostat** to take the temperature of your house **up** to about 80 degrees. When you know you'll be home at say, 6 o'clock, set the timer at 5:30 to take the temperature **down** to 76 or 78 degrees so your home will be cool, and not have a blast of heat hit you like a *flame thrower* when you first open your door.

Before you go to bed (*you know nights are generally cooler than the days*), set it to **raise** the temperature a few degrees. If you program it this way, it can save you money. If you're the type of person who plays "thermostat piano" you know, raise it when you're cool and drop it when you're hot, this **Programmable Thermostat** is your answer.

There are some "if's" that could change the need for one. **If** someone in your household is **home** during the day, of **if** you have kids who come home from school earlier than you, the amount of savings will be **less** because . . . well, **you** can answer that. I can't tell you **everything!** It all depends on your personal situation. **If** you live alone, do it! **If** you have someone home during the day, **why** spend the money?

To **install** one is a piece of cake. Just remove your old manual thermostat. In the back you'll find four wires, all color-coded like a telephone line; match the wires and mount it to the wall. This is a great do-it-yourself project.

Q. I am not a "handy" person. Is there anything simple I can do to make sure my air conditioner is running as efficiently as possible?

A. **Yes!** Even a *Dufuss* can do this, regardless how inept they are at home repair. Keep a clean **filter** in it! A dirty filter can cause as much as ten percent **more** energy usage. If you're using a plain old **fiberglass** filter *(costs a buck or two)* replace it **every four weeks.** If you're using a **Pleated** filter *(my preference),* replace it every two or three **months.** The best way to check is to **look** at it. If it's dirty, replace it and throw out the filter **and** the dirt it collects.

Let me tell you **what** filters do. **Filters do not clean the air in your house!** You **cannot** cure or prevent diseases with **any** type of air-conditioning filter. Don't be taken in by the fads and gimmicks. The **only** thing an air-conditioner **filter** does is . . . **keep dirt out of the air conditioner** to insure it running efficiently.

I don't want to "go to war" against any of these filter manufacturers that **promise you the good** and **frighten you with the bad,** but these new, high-priced AC filters are a **ripoff!** It's amazing what promotion will do for a product. I guess if it's said often enough and loudly enough, **everybody** believes it, perhaps even the **liars** who say all these good things it will **do** and the bad that can happen if you **don't** buy their expensive air filter. It's sad too, because we **want** to believe in a product, don't we? My suggestion; **save your money!**

You might have noticed that I refer to savings on **energy** bills instead of **utility** bills. Energy, to me, means electricity and gas. Utility could include telephone too, huh? So, if you'd like to show off, say "energy bill" a few times and let someone correct you.

Q. **What is the CORRECT TEMPERATURE SETTING for a water heater? Some say keep it as low as 110 degrees, and I've heard others say to keep it as high as 140 degrees?**

A. **Great question!** Most people don't even know what you're talking about. They **assume** that when their heater is connected, it's ready to go, and most of the time it is. But, 110 degrees is like cool man, similar to baby bear's porridge; **too** cold, period! *(Or was it mama bear's porridge?)* It must stay at a **minimum** of 120 degrees! This degree of temperature kills the bacteria. Less than 120 degrees of water temperature could cause you to become sick. Keep it slightly above 120 degrees!

If you have an electric dishwasher, the temperature must then be - 140 degrees! The reason is that the **soap** in the dishwasher will not dissolve unless it is at least that high. Some of the new dishwashers have "pre-heats" to make 120 degrees acceptable.

Q. **My attic is insulated well but my ATTIC STAIRS have no insulation. Should I be concerned?**

A. **No!** There isn't much you **can** do other than **weatherstrip** the opening around the stairs so the trap door closes snugly. You see, when the air conditioner clicks *on* and the fan begins to run, it causes **pressure differences** and will **pull** air through **any** attic crack into your house. Weather-stripping your attic-door opening is relatively simple and inexpensive and a fine do-it-yourself project that helps save you what? **Money!**

Q. **Does my FIREPLACE provide heat for my house?**

A. In most cases, **No!** The fireplace is for looks and romance. Use it to keep your wife happy with soft music, chocolate covered strawberries, a bottle of good wine, and several pillows on a soft comforter when the kids are away. Or for you bachelors and bachlorettes - well, I'm not telling **you** anything you don't already know.

But for heating, I don't think so. You, personally, can heat up your front, then your back if you stand close enough to the open flame and turn around all the time. But actual heat for your house, no. You see, **up** the flue goes the hot air, and **up** the flue goes all your **heated** air from inside your house that your furnace warmed. I'm for the fireplace but, unless you have one designed **especially** for heating *(95 of a 100 aren't)* use it for fun and mood-setting.

Q. **Can CEILING FANS save me money on my energy bill or are they too, just decorator items?**

A.   **Yes,** they can save you a **lot** of money, and they are nice decorator items also. There is a direct relationship between humidity, temperature, and air movement across the skin where human comfort is concerned. This sounds a bit *hi-tech*, I know, but think of it this way.

If you turn a ceiling fan on **medium speed** and you sit under it, you'll feel 4 to 6 degrees **cooler** than the thermostat setting. This means you can set your thermostat several degrees **higher,** use the ceiling fan, enjoy the same degree of comfort, and save about **three** percent on your energy bill each month.

There is a "ceiling" to this, however. You can't set your thermostat to **100 degrees** and expect to save **fifteen percent.** Too high and your **heat** turns on and it becomes a "wash" - plus, major discomfort.

Also, most of these fans have **reverse** on them, and in winter you reverse the pitch of the blades, put your fan on low speed, and this sort of pulls the air **up** and "stirs" the air in the room. Hot air rises quickly in winter, and by mixing, you keep the air more constant which means your furnace will have to run on a **lower** output and you won't **feel** hot air blowing **on** you.

Remember, the **cost** of running a **ceiling fan** is about the same as running a **100-watt light bulb.** They **are** decorative, relaxing, inexpensive to buy, they make you more comfortable, and they **will** save you money.

Q. I was thinking of building a cover over my air-conditioning unit to shade it from the sun, or maybe planting bushes or vines to do the same thing. Will it save me money on my energy bill?

A. **No, don't do that!** These new air-conditioning systems are **meant** to run at very high temperatures. Many are put on buildings in direct view of the sun. What you are referring to is the **Condensing Unit** housed in that large metal box on the outside of your home. This condensing unit must be **free** of all coverings and debris in order to keep good air flow passing across it.

You usually hear the fan **inside** the unit continuously working all summer long. You can hear your neighbor's fan running too, can't you? What this is doing is literally **releasing the heat** that's pulled **out** of the **inside** of the house, to the outside.

This means your AC unit is really a **Heat Pump** in reverse. It takes the heat from **inside** your house, to **outside,** and when the air blows across the coil in the condenser, it releases it to the environment. **No!** Keep that large metal "air conditioner" free of bushes or a cover.

Q. In the summer I have a lot of DIRECT SUNLIGHT coming in my west windows that makes the room unbearably hot, but I like the sun in winter. What can I do to have both, you know, cool in summer but be able to enjoy that warm sun in winter?

A.   Want the best of both worlds, do you? **My** vote goes to these new **sun-screens.** The main objection(s) I get from people is, *"Oh, I've seen those. You can't see through them."* Or, *"They're black, or green; they're ugly!"*

Maybe they **were** ugly, and perhaps difficult or impossible to see through but, they've had a major **facelift.** The **new** sun-screen of the 90's looks **no different** than any **ordinary** screen on your windows, and they **are** terrific.

Manufacturers recognized the demand by the American public for efficiency **and** looks. There are several companies who make them, or you can go to a home improvement center, buy the components, and make them yourself.

In summer, these sun-screens block about **seventy** percent of the *Ultraviolet Rays* of the sun. In the winter, take them down and let the sunshine in, face it with a grin. Smiler's never lose, frowner's never win. Just let the . . . Sorry! I got carried away for a moment on that fun, upbeat song. I highly recommend sun-screens. The cost is very reasonable. In my opinion, it is one of the **best** options for a homeowner to buy.

I need to warn you against . . . **tinting!** Tinting is expensive and it can be quite unattractive on a home. Keep the tinting for commercial buildings and your car windows and windshield.

Q. **I am afraid my pipes will freeze in the winter. I'd like to insulate them. Will this also save money on my energy bill?**

A. **No,** not much savings on your energy bill, but **big** savings on your plumbing bill, your cleanup bill and possibly on a large bill for **furniture replacement.** If a pipe should freeze and break, the damage is horrendous. Wrap 'em if they're in attics, walls, or outside and exposed. Insulating your pipes in winter is extremely important - on the *hot,* as well as on the *cold* side. To do it right, follow this procedure carefully.

There are copper, galvanized, and *PVC* pipes used for hot and cold water. Since *PVC* is not accepted by larger cities' building code, I'll talk only about copper and galvanized. The most common size for both is half and three-quarter inches. Most of the pipes are in your attic. If the insulation is loose-fitting, the air will cause the pipes to sweat **inside** that insulation during certain times of the year and literally **destroy** the pipes. A tight fit is what you want.

In applying this insulation, you can use one of two things to tie it down; **Nylon Tie Wraps** every few feet or, **Metal Duct Tape . . . not** the old plastic duct tape, it will come apart in the attic. In fact, I don't know **how** they get away with calling this plastic stuff **duct** tape. Get the special **metal tape** used for duct work with a backing that you peel off. It looks like foil and is ideal for wrapping pipes in the attic, basement or outside.

Metal Duct Tape . . . not the old plastic duct tape, it will come apart in the attic. In fact, I don't know **how** they get away with calling this plastic stuff, **D**uct Tape. Get the special **metal tape** used for duct work with a backing that you peel off. It looks like foil and is ideal for wrapping pipes in the attic, basement or outside.

As far as saving **big** money on your energy bill, I doubt it! But, hot water will stay hotter **longer** in winter. In the summer, this wrapping keeps the heat from the hot water pipes from radiating into your house. So it **could** save some energy-bill money because of those factors.

* * * * *

So, my friends, this was the last answer I have to share with you in **this** book. I hope you enjoyed it and that it helps make home repair easier and more fun for you. I **guarantee** it will save you money! Listen to my show on **NEWSRADIO 740 KTRH** and call **(526-4740)** any Saturday or Sunday between 11 AM and 2 PM if you have a problem with anything involving home repair. Watch my TV show on **KHOU TV (Channel 11 Houston)** each Saturday from 5:30 to 6:00 PM, and look for my **follow-up books** that will go into greater detail on specific areas of home improvement.

IMPORTANT TIPS TO REMEMBER

Many of my suggestions cost **nothing,** other than **checking** on various things. A little **time** is worth, what could be, major expense! Here's some **re-**reminders:

* When working with **electrical fixtures,** make certain the power is *OFF*, either at the switch box or fuse box, whichever applies.

* Get those leaves and pine needles **off** that roof. Takes maybe 15 minutes.

* When using a **tall** ladder, check the rungs and the angle. For a **Step Ladder,** open it **all the way!** **Don't** step on the top rung and please, do not try to step on the part that comes out, you know, where you put the paint bucket.

* Don't *chinch* on cheap paint. It'll cost you in the long haul.

* Take a leisurely stroll around your home at least a few times a year and **look** for those **termite houses**. If you see one, call the exterminator **immediately!** I'm not for destroying anyone's home but treat **termites** like a burglar. They are **un**invited guests.

*   Spend the few bucks for a tube of **caulk** and get those windows and cracks filled to save on your air conditioning and heating bill. It works.

*   **Call** the person who just sold you that ceiling fan if you're not certain which wires go where. White on white, black on black, green on green. I've seen **some** fans with light attachments, where they slip in an additional wire or two. Call and ask! Takes only a few minutes.

*   When your plumber visits you for **any** reason, have him **show you** where the temperature adjustment is on your **water** heater. (Remember, it's a **water** heater and not a **hot** water heater. It isn't necessary to **heat** water that is **already hot!**)

*   In fact, if **any** repairman comes out *(or repair**woman**)* ask them questions if you're not certain where or what something is. A little knowledge can go a long way.

*   **Continuous Ridge Vents** are the only way to go to insure proper ventilation. Too, if you have a tree **limb** rubbing on your roof, cut it before it eats a hole right through.

*   Be **wary** of any person who solicits **Home Improvement** at your door or over the telephone. Don't sign **anything** unless you consult your attorney, a relative who is a contractor, or **me!** There is a 3-day "right of recision" but to be smart, **don't** sign! It **could** cost you your home!

MEN

I've been fortunate to have **NEVER** received a letter from a man *(or a woman)* telling me that my advice was wrong! You all know I take great pride in my work, and that I keep current on new happenings. But, **men** don't always follow my advice to the letter as do women. And many men have found a **short-cut** to some things. What I'd appreciate, **men,** is if you **do** find a better way, call me and I'll **share it with the world!**

* * * * *

TOM TYNAN is available for personal appearances, luncheons, banquets, home shows, seminars, etc. He is entertaining and informative. Call **(713) 388-2547** for cost and availability.

* * * * *

For a copy(s) of *Home Improvement with Tom Tynan,* send a personal check or money order in the amount of $12.85 for each book to: **SWAN PUBLISHING, 126 Live Oak, Suite 100, Alvin, TX 77511.** Please allow 7-10 days for delivery. Or, to order by **VISA, MC** or **AMEX,** call: **(713) 268-6776, (713) 388-2547 or long distance, dial 1-800-TOM-TYNAN.**

LIBRARIES - BOOKSTORES
QUANTITY ORDERS:

SWAN PUBLISHING
126 Live Oak, Suite 100
Alvin, TX 77511

Call (713) 388-2547
or FAX (713) 585-3738